Don't
Get
Mad–
Get
Even

Don't Get Mad– Get Even

The Fine Art of Revengemanship

Jane Inder and Hilary Eyre

Paladin Press · Boulder, Colorado

Don't Get Mad—Get Even
The Fine Art of Revengemanship
by Jane Inder and Hilary Eyre

Copyright © 1994 by Jane Inder and Hilary Eyre

ISBN 0-87364-796-3
Printed in the United States of America

Published by Paladin Press, a division of
Paladin Enterprises, Inc.
Gunbarrel Tech Center
7077 Winchester Circle
Boulder, Colorado 80301 USA
+1.303.443.7250

Direct inquiries and/or orders to the above address.

Visit our Web site at www.paladin-press.com

Contents

Introduction

A friend of a friend spends his days dicing with
death on the overcrowded roads of London's
urban jungle as a motorcycle courier. He told us this
story of a colleague who one afternoon received a call
on his radio for a job going from an address in
Notting Hill to a high-street bank in the centre of the
West End and back. It was a routine enough request,
and the courier fired up his bike and headed off.

Within 10 minutes, he pulled up outside the
Notting Hill address and was given a manila business envelope and a holdall. He duly stuffed the two
items in his back box and roared off toward the West
End. At the bank he did as instructed and handed
over the envelope to the cashier along with the
holdall. Within seconds of the woman's reading the
note, however, alarms went off and the place was
overrun with security guards, all pointing their guns
at the hapless biker.

Stunned, he was handcuffed and bundled into the
back of a police van. Later, in the police station, he
was shown the message he had delivered in the enve-

lope. It read: "I have a gun and am not afraid to use it. Fill the bag with money."

Bank robbery by proxy? No, it was a classic case of revenge. Six months earlier our hulking, leather-clad despatch rider had crossed a fellow biker in love. Not content with stealing his colleague's girlfriend, it seemed he had also light-fingered a few of his spare parts. Unfortunately, though, he didn't reckon on the power of positive revenge.

Like the patient avenger of this story, just about everyone has been dumped on at some time or another, but not everyone manages to even the score quite so satisfyingly. There's a strong tradition among the British to simply accept whatever dirt people, companies, bureaucracies, government officials—whoever—dish out. "Turn the other cheek", we're told. "Don't make waves."

Trouble is, the meek won't inherit the earth; they'll just get ground into it. The way we see it, in this life you have two choices: either lie down and be a victim or stand up and be what you want. This book is designed to give those of you who are sick of being the victim a chance to settle the score in the old eye-for-an-eye tradition.

THE 10 COMMANDMENTS OF REVENGE

Follow these rules faithfully and you'll destroy your target without leaving yourself open to attack.

I. Never trust or confide in anyone. It's the quickest way to lose friends and make new enemies, as even your closest, most trustworthy chum can accidentally let things slip—or turn traitor. And never be tempted to gloat, no matter how successful you are at getting even. There's no surer way for you to be found out.

II. Never use your own telephone for revenge business. Always use a public telephone or that of a secondary target so the calls cannot be traced back to you or anyone who knows you.

III. Never use your home address. Secure a mailbox in a false name or that of a secondary target in another part of town so nothing can ever be traced back to you.

IV. Never touch revenge documents or any of your target's possessions with your bare hands. Paper—and that means letters, envelopes, etc.—will hold your fingerprints, so make sure you wear gloves.

V. Never rush things. You need time to cool off. Also, preparation is nine-tenths of any plan's success. You need to have thought of all the angles and be ready with a contingency plan, and you can't do that overnight. Then there's the fact that if you want to keep your hit anonymous, no matter what your target has done to you, you need to give him or her time to forget all about you if you don't want him to put two and two together and come up with your name.

VI. Learn all there is to know about your target, and never take that person lightly, no matter how thick you'd like to think he or she is. Find out as much as you can: address, birth date, and telephone numbers; names of partners, friends, and relatives; bank details; place of work. Go through rubbish bins if you have to—even the most insignificant-seeming piece of information can help. And the best revenge plots are hatched by people who know their target—and his or her weaknesses—even better than the target does.

VII. Always pay cash for items used in your revenge schemes. Never use cheques or credit cards or any form of payment that can be traced back to you.

VIII. Never buy equipment for schemes from people who know you. Go to another town and spread your purchases around.

IX. Never threaten your victim before carrying out your plan. Why offer a warning that you intend to settle the score? When bad things start to happen to him, chances are your target will remember your threat and, instead of evening the score, you'll find you've scored yourself an own goal. Likewise, never admit responsibility, even if your target confronts you, and never, ever succumb to an attack of the guilts and apologize. Firm up that stiff upper lip and adopt the Foreign Office motto: "Never apologize. Never explain."

X. Never leave evidence lying around, however circumstantial it might seem. As Francois de La Rochefoucauld wrote in *Maximes*, "The height of cleverness is to be able to conceal it." Keep everything well-hidden and preferably somewhere other than your home or workplace. Secure a safety deposit box in a false name to hide the evidence if necessary. And that includes this book!

IMPORTANT: The schemes, plots, plans, and conspiracies outlined in these pages are presented *for entertainment purposes only*. It is not our intention that you use this book as a manual, and we certainly don't expect that anyone reading it would ever actually carry out any of the stunts described. The book is intended to give readers a vicarious thrill as they imagine carrying out the pranks themselves. We wouldn't want you to think we actually advocate going out and being deliberately unpleasant to someone else or that we are suggesting that you act in an illegal manner.

Advertising

*D*esperately seeking retribution? The small ads can be a big help in bringing down a foe. Few would dispute the power of advertising, certainly not the multinationals that have enabled Charles Saatchi to become this country's best-known collector of contemporary art, nor the conglomerates who started admen like Ridley Scott and Alan Parker on their illustrious film-making careers. Okay, maybe you can't afford to hire the Saatchi brothers to tell the world what a scumbag your enemy is, but you *can* harness the power of the media in your own small way.

MONEY FOR OLD ROPE?

Set your target up in business. Place an ad in the local paper offering cash for bottle tops, old newspapers, empty tin cans or any other useless junk you can think of. Make the prices attractive—say, 5p for each bottle top or old newspaper—and leave your target's home address. You can be very sure he'll do thriving business at those rates. While you're at it, you might like to make some handbills to put through nearby letter-boxes. Leave a small pile of bills on the table in the local library, then sit back and think about the bills your target is going to be getting when all those eager people come knocking at his door with their sacks full of rubbish.

Maybe you think your target's more of a seller than a buyer. Well, everybody loves a bargain, so won't your man (or woman) be the popular one when he offers free, house-trained Rottweiler puppies to give away . . . or a Harley-Davidson at half its real value ("urgent debt needs to be repaid") . . . or even guns. Try to pick items that will appeal to the kind of people who aren't very patient about being messed around. Actually, if somebody passed the gun advert on to the police, they would probably be interested, too . . .

DOCTOR IN TROUBLE

There are other areas of business in which you might like to make the punishment fit the crime. For example, if you've been done over by a doctor, give him the treatment by placing an advert for cut-price abortions performed "at home". Or maybe the slimy accountant who messed up your tax return would care to advertise his services under the heading: "Never Pay Tax Again". As a responsible citizen, you would be only right and proper to pass these unsavoury notices on to the relevant authorities.

If a particular shop deserves it, you might like to

get some special car stickers made up singing the shop's praises. Be prepared to invest in quality—the sticker must be waterproof and hard-wearing, and if the glue doesn't seem quite strong enough, get a tube of superglue. Then go out on the town sticking your target's promotional stickers all over the bonnets of the most expensive cars you can find.

Sticker blitzes such as this are also effective against politicians. Just call party headquarters for as many stickers as they will send you, then spread liberally over people's private property to ensure a very sticky situation for your candidate.

PIZZA EXCESS

Dialling out for pizza is one of the more civilised customs we've inherited from the Americans, although the competition where we live is really starting to hot up. Most weeks we get at least one leaflet through the door offering new, better toppings for less money. The problem is, often when we get in after a late night out, they've all shut up shop and gone home.

So just imagine what a success your target would be if he did a leaflet drop all over the neighbourhood offering to deliver pizza 24 hours a day at half the price of the competition. Maybe you could even throw in a special offer to start—two pizzas for the price of one, plus a free litre bottle of Coke. What a winner! Of course, that phone just wouldn't stop, especially after all the other outlets shut up shop for the night. Top that!

SPREAD A LITTLE HAPPINESS . . .

Another service your target may wish to offer is that of escort agent. Let your fingers do the walking as far as your Yellow Pages and place an ad on his or her behalf under "Escorts". Once again, that 24-hour service is essential, as are lots of erotic hints about the special services the "Sisters of Abundant Delectation" can offer their customers. As the Yellow Pages are only updated once a year, you can expect this one to run and run—and for your target to join it.

While we're on the subject of sex, your target could also advertise for new friends in any number of "adult" magazines. It's surprising what you can find on the top shelf at your local newsagent. Browse around and see if you can find a publication that will really reflect your target's tastes. It's amazing the variety there are for speciality interests, and your target's special preference might be for older women, fat women, women with enormous breasts—or men.

A good friend who is gay has had tremendous response to ads placed in various "pink" magazines, as well as some surprising insertions: anatomically unlikely pictures, locks of curly, rather coarse-looking hair, and some very descriptive letters. Ads of this kind usually require that you pay for a post-office box, so use a postal order, not a cheque, and put it in your target's name—but with a slight error in the address, so that those eager, open pen-pals' letters get sent to your target's nosy neighbour by mistake.

A variation on this theme is to place an ad in a gay

magazine proudly announcing that your target has "come out". The ad should be an admission that the person only married for "cover" and is now proud to admit to being gay. The lover who has inspired this refreshing change of attitude should also be mentioned. Pick an uptight neighbour, friend, or colleague. Naturally, you will buy whichever edition this announcement runs in—and send anonymous photocopies to all and sundry.

SMOKED SALMAN

If your target is of a literary bent, employ one of our leading authors to throw the book at him. A nice, prominent advertisement offering signed copies of Salman Rushdie's *Satanic Verses* would have a sure-fire response, especially if you selected a newspaper with a high Muslim readership—the *Telegraph & Argus* in Bradford, perhaps. This works particularly effectively if your target runs a book shop.

While you're thinking along these lines, you could also extend your target's hospitality to "fellow sympathisers". Perhaps your ad could also invite like-minded people to a discussion group on lifting "this absurd and stupid *fatwah* against Salman Rushdie". Or maybe you can think or some other kind of meeting that would be particularly appropriate to your target's home: a gay-rights discussion group for a bigot, an African Awareness Society for a racist, or a "swingers" experimental group for fully paid-up members of the Moral Majority.

SHOP TACTICS

Shop windows are also ideal spots to place ads cheaply, though you may need to persuade a friend who is not known in the neighbourhood to go in on your behalf. Some big stores even have a free notice board where you can just post notices of your own. An ad to the effect of *"FOR SALE: complete contents of luxury home. Everything must go—occupier going abroad"* would tend to have a particularly negative effect on the target's spouse. Alternatively, perhaps you can think of a worthy recipient for some of the following:

"WANTED: Attractive young men for modelling sessions. Good fees paid."
"WANTED: Very young girls and boys for art photographs. Pets also welcome. Good fees paid to children with talent."
"Soiled underwear needed for psychology experiment. Please send, with background and social details, to . . ."
"Confidential AIDS testing. Send or bring a blood or urine sample to . . ."

As a variation, you may prefer to put your target's name on the advertisement with the address of his or her next-door neighbour. This should ensure that your target is the subject of lively debate around town.

DEAD FUNNY

Send in an obituary to the local paper in your target's name. List his achievements in a genuine and plausible way, and explain how his untimely death as the result of an accident (pick a suitable means for your target's destruction) is a terrible tragedy for his friends and family. If the paper phones to check the details, your target will be freaked out. If they don't call and it gets published, he will be doubly freaked out when he reads the torn-out page that you have posted to him anonymously. His horror, in fact, will be eclipsed only by the distraught phone calls he gets from his friends, telling him they've been invited to his wake and sent photocopies of his obituary.

YOU'RE THE ONE THAT I WANT . . .

Turn your target into a wanted man—or woman. You'll need a full-face photograph, and some alarmist copy warning shopkeepers and customers to be on the look-out for this notorious thief and con artist. Your target's name should feature large and should be augmented by a brief, plausible outline of his or her criminal career. Sign it the local community's merchant's association. Print up posters using a trusted local printer or a friend with access to a fairly sophisticated home computer and, taking care that you are unobserved, distribute prominently around town.

In a similar vein, you could put up posters warning others that your target's business is a rip-off outfit. This is satisfyingly simple and quite effective.

ALL THE RIGHT CARDS

Though it is not strictly advertising, some people

like to leave their business cards pinned on notice boards in the hope of attracting work. With this in mind, you might like to have some cards made up on your target's behalf. The great thing about business cards is that these days you don't even need to walk into a printer's to get them made. There are machines at various large main-line stations (the last one I saw was at Victoria) that will print about 70 official-looking black-and-white business cards for just a few pounds. Imagine the services your target might offer: colonic irrigation (discounts for pensioners), stripper-grams, black magic, and voodoo.

Or play it absolutely straight. Make up cards listing your target's name and genuine job and place of work, then go out on the town, get very drunk, make lots of new friends—prostitutes, tramps, boring old farts—and press your card on them, insisting they call you tomorrow. Offer to lend them money, invite them to come over for dinner. You will find these cards an absolute godsend whenever you are forced to identify yourself to someone you'd really rather have nothing to do with, and your target will be mystified as to the identity of his or her "evil twin".

BLACK MARKS

If you've been at the receiving end of some rude treatment by a shopkeeper, spread the word. Make up some little signs, and when the creep in question isn't looking, post one in the window and leave others lying around the shop. The message should be to the effect of, *"Warning: If your skin is darker or your religion different from mine, DO NOT SHOP IN*

MY STORE!" Not only will this discourage customers, it will probably prompt a visit from the police who are, quite rightly, rather sensitive about racial issues these days.

SHOW HOME FROM HELL

Have you ever received one of those leaflets through the door offering you the chance to get your windows replaced, roof retiled, or drive repaved at a discount rate in return for becoming a "show home" for six months? We've never paid much attention to them, but we can only imagine the discount must be pretty good to put up with having an enormous placard obscuring the view from your front window for months on end.

However, if you've ever been ridden over roughshod by some cowboy who's left your front garden looking like Salisbury Plain, you can turn this business practice to your own advantage. If Mr. Cowboy won't do the decent thing and clear up his mess once he's been paid, make a sign of your own to the the effect of "Landscaping by (name of cowboy outfit and telephone number)". While you're at it, you might like to drive around and find other examples of urban blight for which you can give your dodgy operator full credit. With luck, he will do the decent thing and clean up his act.

Animals

*M*an's best friend . . . or a howling nuisance? The British are well known for their soppy attitude to all things warm and furry with cold noses. In fact, per capita, Britain has the largest population of pets in Europe, with more than 14 million dogs and cats and 1.5 million budgies. Many of them are delightful—loyal and loving friends. But sometimes, thanks usually to their selfish owners, they can make your hackles rise. And when that happens, it's time to get even.

MAKE THE FUR FLY

Use your target's pooch or puss to convey your heartfelt sentiments. Type out an anonymous note saying exactly what you think of your target and attach it to his or her pet's collar.

SOMETHING FISHY

Animals can be your allies, of course. Entice the

neighbourhood cats into your taget's garden with a liberal sprinkling of oriental fish sauce, or encourage dogs to dig up the flower beds by seeding them with chunks of meat.

BARKING MAD

Lots of dogs howl all day long, stopping magically as soon as their owners come home in the evening. If that's your problem, give your target a blast of what it's like by buying a dog whistle. The sound, inaudible to humans, should set his canine's canines on edge and have him howling in a jiffy.

HAVE A FIELD-DAY

If your target's a farmer or has a few large animals, get your revenge by turning his or her home into a pigsty, literally. Simply herd a few of his prize porkers, dairy cows, or sheep into the house and shut them in. Leave a sink full of water for them, of course, if they're not likely to be discovered for awhile.

BUG THEM

Lots of people keep insects as pets—so why not introduce this delightful hobby to a target who has yet to discover the fun you can have with a six-legged friend? Give him a real buzz by delivering a consignment of live bees. You can buy them in boxes from apiarists. Introduce them, carefully, through the letter-box of your target's home. Oh, and make sure you sting your target for the bill, too.

Cockroaches, earwigs, and woodlice are also easy to come by. Collect them up and either post them to your target first class or release them into his home or office. Then deliver the killer blow by dropping a business card for a firm of exterminators through the door.

ONE FOR THE RATBAGS

They say that in London you are never more than 80 feet away from a rat—of the four-legged variety, that is. Numbers decrease outside the capital, but, wherever you are, you can be sure there's something brown, furry, and rodentlike not too far away.

Usually, though, we're protected from seeing the voracious little beasts by virtue of the fact that they tend to operate undercover—under manhole covers, in fact. Yes, the nation's sewage system is the great breeding ground for Britain's teeming rat population.

So if your target's a member of the two-legged species and you would like to give him a chance to meet his cousins, introductions are an easy matter. Many homes have a manhole cover in the garden. All you need do to let loose the local rat horde is shift the manhole cover slightly. The rats, once liberated, will infest your target's house—they're amazingly adept at breaking in—and, with luck, your target's neighbours', too, wreaking havoc and leaving their unmistakable little brown calling cards all over the place.

From there, it will usually be a job for the council exterminators, but, until they go to work, you'll have the satisfaction of knowing that at least one dirty rat has got what he deserves.

Rats and mice can also be used to great effect in restaurants and other establishments, such as butchers, where hygiene is paramount but you've found the owners don't mind dishing the dirt on you. Catch yourself a generously sized rat (or, failing that, a couple of mice). How you do it is up to you, but be gentle—you want your quarry fighting-fit when you finally get round to liberating it in your target's premises.

It should be a simple matter to take the rodent into your chosen restaurant in a box inside a bag. Place the bag under your table and, when you're ready—perhaps just before the bill arrives—loosen the lid of the box so the rat or mice can escape. When they do, scream, point, stand on your chair, and let everybody know what a hideous, monstrous rat you've just seen. Choose a busy night for maximum effect, and threaten to inform the council's health inspector.

Can't find a live rodent? Well, a dead one can be used to great effect, too. Either dump the corpse just as you are leaving so some other lucky diner finds it, or, for a time-delay effect, dump the body in a glass jar, add 2 inches of water, and screw the lid on tightly. Deposit the jar in an out-of-the-way place where it's unlikely to be discovered for a couple of days at least—in a planter, perhaps, or behind a dresser. Decaying organic matter, such as a dead rat, releases a lot of noxious gases which, eventually, will build up enough pressure to explode the jar. Messy, messy, messy, and so appropriate—rat stink for a real rat fink.

RETURN TO SENDER

Here's a rather more sophisticated variation on the dog (or cat) turd through the letter-box trick. Next time your target's pooch or puss deposits its little pile in your garden, have handy a pretty gift box stuffed with a cosy bed of shredded tissue paper. Now, add the crap, and then another layer of packing, put on the lid, wrap it up, address it to your target, and post it off. Your greedy target will root around in the packing looking for her present and instead find something distinctly unpleasant. What a good way to land her in the shit.

TAKE THE PISS

If you're sick of the neighbours' cats or dogs marking your garden as their territory with hefty sprays of urine, get your own back with a drop or 10 of yours. Collect it and decant it into a spray bottle, then give the offending owners' doors, cars, whatever, a good squirt when the opportunity presents itself. Oh, and a bit of food selectivity the night before you commence this activity can improve the potency of your home brew: try drinking beer with asparagus for a truly distinctive aroma. An added bonus is that the animal whose territory you have just "marked" will then try to re-mark its territory with a spray of its own, doubling the impact of your initial hit.

LAY THE BAIT

Laying poisoned baits for annoying animals is strictly off the sophisticated revengster's agenda. You don't want to murder the animal, just make life murder for the poor unfortunate's owner. Here's what you do: toss bite-sized balls of plain, unadulterated mince over the target's fence, along with an empty box of rat poison. The idea is to create the illusion that someone is trying to bait the dog or cat. Hopefully, the owner will run up an expensive veterinary bill making sure that his mangy mutt or moggy has not eaten poison. The animal, of course, will be fine, but you can bet your target will be feeling decidedly sick at the end of it all.

HUE AND CRY

If your target's one of that strange species of animal owners that lives for the show ring, why not put her pampered little bundles of pride and joy out of action for a while with a little judicious grooming?

Fill a bottle with a fine misting spray attachment with a strong solution of food colouring. Now you need to get hold of the prize pooch and give its coat a thorough going over. Try several different colours for a rainbow effect (harmless to the animal but guaranteed to make your target see red. Alternatively, if your target favours longhaired breeds, clip them, or clip a suitably brief message into their fur.

Another way to get at your prize-hungry target is by popping along to one of the dog shows she's entered. Take along your trusty dog whistle and, when your target's dog is in the ring, just give a little whistle. The dog will go crazy, the judges will decide the champ has turned into a chump, and your target will go home empty-handed.

Or you can take advantage of Mother Nature to achieve your ends—simply by helping a stray stud get his end in. It's amazing how hot and bothered pedigree pet owners get if their pristine darling escapes while she's in heat, and how appalled they are when they find her coupled with the local brute.

KICK UP A STINK

If your target's dog is one of those poor, miserable creatures that never gets enough exercise and is forced by its lazy master or mistress to spend a lot of time indoors, one good way to let the owner know what a stinker you think he is would be to feed the animal hard-boiled eggs. The next day the owner should find himself longing for a breath of fresh air, and if that doesn't encourage him to give the doggy a bit more exercise, nothing will.

FINE KETTLE OF FISH

Fish are prime targets for tipping the scales of justice in your favour. All manner of substances, when added to the tank or pond, will leave the inhabitants belly up and your target looking green about the gills. A copper penny in a salt-water tank, for example, will turn the fish into floaters and leave your target gasping, while a strong solution of gelatin in the goldfish bowl will turn the residents into an impressive fish-in-aspic dish.

A handful or 10 of wallpaper paste will achieve the same effect in a pond, by all accounts, and will give your target something to carp about. Or you can try doctoring the fish food with tissue paper soaked in drain cleaner and then dried and shredded to resemble those coloured floating flakes. For a time-delay effect, if you've got other fish to fry, sabotage the aquarium thermostat.

Of course, you could always use nature to achieve your ends. Introduce an aggressive species such as a Siamese fighting fish and leave it to turn the aquarium's more docile denizens into fish fingers.

JUICY LITTLE MORSELS

One of the advantages of fish, apart from the fact that they don't bark, is that you can eat them. In fact, some species of ornamental fish—koi, for example—also make good, if extremely expensive, eating. Imagine how delightful it would be to serve up your target's prime £1,000 koi—deftly filleted and pan-fried—to him or her. Of course, your target need never know; you could just savour the situation quietly. Or you could round off the meal with a tiny coffin bearing the inedible but identifiable remains.

For those less adept in the kitchen, goldfish fit neatly between two slices of bread. Add some lettuce and a dab of mayonnaise, and it's goldfish-to-go.

If you can't quite bring yourself to go fishing, you can always fake it. Get a good-sized carrot or a chunk of turnip and whittle yourself a goldfish-size sculpture. Keep it in your pocket until you're near your target's bowl or aquarium, then pull it out and dump it in the water. Plunge your hand in, fish around, and pull it out, waving it around a bit to make it look like it's wriggling, then pop it in your mouth. Watch the rush for the bathroom as something other than outrage bubbles up inside your target.

Of course, if you're really serious—and a serious sashimi fan, too—you could forget the carrot or turnip and just go for the fish.

GET THEM COLLARED

This trick is pretty horrible, but then we never said we were in the game of being nice. You will need a fresh cat or dog corpse (the road-killed variety rather than a DIY one, please), a collar, and a length of strong string. Put the collar round the corpse's neck, tie one end of the string to it, and secure the other end around your target's bumper bar. Hide the ex-moggy or doggy under the car. Hopefully your target won't see the corpse before driving off . . . but everyone else will. And the police and the RSPCA should take such obvious cruelty deadly seriously. What a drag . . .

BODY OF EVIDENCE

Road casualties can come in handy in other ways, too. Get yourself a nice, fresh animal corpse and, once again, tie a piece of string around its neck. Now, position the body on one side of the road along the route your target usually takes home from work. Position yourself, holding the free end of the string on the other and lie doggo until your target drives up. As he does, pull hard on the string to drag the animal across in front of him.

At this point, you need to make sure you have positioned yourself so that if the target swerves, you don't end up in the same condition as your stiff little friend. If your target is half-way decent (although, let's face it, given that he's got himself on your hit list, he's probably not), he'll stop and be freaked out by the carnage he's just caused. If not, you'll at least have the satisfaction of knowing you've given him a nasty shock—and something even nastier to clean off his car.

If your dear, departed pooch or puss obviously wasn't leash-trained in its former life and proves resistant to being tugged across the road, consider mounting it on a skateboard. The corpse will tip off when hit and you should be able to reel in the skate and make your getaway unobserved as your target screeches to halt—if only to check whether there's any damage to the car.

Note: if you can't find a dead cat or dog, consider the merits of a mothy old stuffed one. Imagine the surprise on your target's face when he discovers what just crossed his path. Now that should knock the stuffing right out of him.

PIGS MIGHT FLY

Okay, so that might be overstretching it, but it is possible to make cats and hedgehogs and all manner of smaller animals fly through the air with the greatest of ease. But not when they're alive. What you need is one (or more) of those flattened corpses that have been run over so many times they look like one of those split and boned ducks that are hung inside the windows of Chinese restaurants and sun-dried till they're just as crispy. The result is a surprisingly aerodynamic weapon that will sail through the air with the grace and accuracy of a frisbee wherever you might happen to want to send it. If you're a poor frisbee spinner, of course, you can always rely on the Royal Mail to make sure your message gets through. A jiffy bag and a first-class stamp should be all it takes to send it winging on its way to your target.

NOSY PARKERS

If you're troubled by police and sniffer dogs searching your home at various inconvenient times, it pays to know that a liberal dousing of bleach, ammonia, or smelling salts on the floor will wipe their supersensitive snozzes right out for a few days.

MORTAL COIL

The mere mention of the word snake is enough to give some people the screaming heebie-jeebies, so imagine what fun you could have with one. Specialist pet magazines list suppliers, and some pet shops sell snakes. Pythons are particularly popular, but be warned—they don't come cheap. Once you have secured your snake, you will need to introduce it to your target. Try the laundry basket, under the duvet, the interior of the car, or a desk drawer in the office. Discovery should be enough to make even that hardened snake in the grass change his ways.

Should your own courage fail you in handling the real thing, there are a variety of convincingly realistic fake snakes around (try joke shops), as well as the option of snakes that have suffered a visit to the taxidermist. Of course, you could also perform this scam using lizards or any of the bigger, more terrifying forms of insect life. Once again, for sources, see the small ads at the back of exotic pet magazines.

DOGGED DETERMINATION

Place an advert in your local free newspaper in your target's name. Say you are offering a £100 reward for whoever finds "your son's beloved Rover". Give a vague description, bearing in mind that German shepherds, Labradors, and Jack Russells are the most common breeds in the UK, and ask anyone who finds Rover to come to your (target's) address after 7 P.M.

TAILS BETWEEN THEIR LEGS

We've all met dogs whose idea of fun is attacking anyone who happens to walk on their patch of pavement. If you've got one of these brutes in your neighbourhood, it pays to pack a pistol—a water pistol, that is. Fill it with water if you're feeling kind, lemon or onion juice or a solution of Tabasco sauce and water if the miserable cur has made you bitter. And remember, don't shoot till you see the whites of their eyes. Guaranteed to turn those testosterone-laden territorial terrorists into stay-at-home sourpusses.

UNBRIDLED PASSION

If your target's a member of the horsey set, give free reign to your anger by sabotaging his tack. A couple of good-sized spiny burs on the underside of the saddle blanket should buck its nag up no end—and throw up a few surprises for your target when he mounts. What better way to let him know someone thinks he's a real prick?

HOUNDED OUT

Finally, if your gripe is with someone close to home—your flatmate or partner's canine—why not speed your quest to have it re-homed with a little sacrifice on your part? Take an item of your clothing and rip it up a little. Now put it in Fido's basket and make sure your flatmate finds it first. When presented with the evidence of Fido's bad behaviour, affect upset, but don't lay it on too thick. Repeat with another item of your clothing, then again with something belonging to Fido's owner. If that doesn't land the mutt in the doghouse, then obviously your flatmate/partner is as thick as his or her best friend and you're barking up the wrong tree. Move out.

At Home

It's a sad fact of life that most accidents happen in the home, yet, for some strange reason, we continue to believe that once the front door is closed behind us and we are safely indoors, nothing can harm us. And that's what makes your target's home one of the best places for sabotage. There are myriad ways you can lay your plans—and you can exact your revenge in just about any room in the house. Here are a few ideas to help you keep the home fires of revenge burning.

BLACK LOOK

Get hold of a few small pieces of graphite or a spoonful or so of graphite dust (you should be able to buy this from a good hardware store as a form of solid lubricant). Now you need to gain access to your target's shower. Remove the shower head—in most cases, it simply unscrews—and dry the inside as best you can. Slip the graphite in and screw the head back in place. Next time your target uses the shower, the graphite will cover him or her from head to toe in black graphite solution—and create an awful mess in the shower to boot.

No graphite? Well, soup up the shower by substituting a couple of Oxo cubes. Or you could add a block of solid poster paint if your really want to bring a little colour to her dull, grey life.

Any of these methods could also be used successfully to sabotage the executive showers at your workplace—a sort of dirty-tricks campaign.

TENDER TOUCH

While you're in the bathroom, why not top up her box of Radox or whatever bath salts she uses with a couple of tins of meat tenderiser. Don't worry, it's an entirely natural substance, made from tropical papaya. The only thing is, after a couple of minutes of wallowing, your target will begin to feel like she's steeping in a bath of horse liniment—and she'll have a burning desire to leap into an icy-cold plunge pool.

BRUSH WITH FATE

Moving to the sink, have handy a syringe and either garlic oil or, at a pinch, a tube of garlic paste. Suck up a syringe-full and inject it into your target's toothpaste. Put the cap back on and squish the tube around a bit to mix the oil and toothpaste. Alternatively, add the oil to his bottle of mouthwash. Now, that's bound to leave a bad taste in his mouth.

THIN END OF THE WEDGE

Do your target a good turn by helping him stick to that diet he's always moaning about. Run a bead of superglue around the rubber door seal of the refrigerator and, while you're at it, around the pantry door. Just think of all the pounds he'll lose paying to have the fridge gasket replaced.

FLUSHED WITH SUCCESS

Toilets are a prime target for masters of revenge. One of the most effective, albeit crude, methods of dumping on your target is that practised by many a local authority in their bid to discourage squatters from taking over vacant properties: stopping them squatting, literally, by cementing up the bog. Here's how to do it: turn off the water supply to the toilet, then flush it twice. That should empty the bowl. Now dump a load of freshly mixed concrete down it—either fill it completely or use just enough to plug the s–bend. Expanding insulation foam will also do the trick nicely.

If cement or expanding foam seems a little bit obvious and you like more subtle hits, try bunging the s-bend with a dishcloth. Shove it as far back as possible and wad it in nice and tight. The advantage of this is that when the target next flushes her loo, the water will back up and possibly overflow. Even if it doesn't, she'll still be faced with having to stick her arm in a soup of effluvia to get at the problem—or call out a plumber.

A sophisticated variation on the old clingfilmunder-the-seat and-stretched-across-the-bowl trick is to have a piece of Plexiglas cut to fit the bowl dimensions exactly (the lower down the better). Next time your target has to go, he'll find his waste has nowhere to go—unless he reaches down and sorts out the problem manually.

Alternatively, why not unseat him by slapping a liberal coating of matching high-gloss enamel paint on the toilet seat—and neglecting to put up the "Wet Paint" sign? What a loo-ser.

IN THE SHIT

On the subject of sanitary matters, if your target has a septic tank, you can sabotage him in all sorts of ways. The time-honoured favourite is dumping household bleach down it. This destroys the delicate balance of bacteria needed to break down the waste, with the result that the tank simply won't work and will have to be pumped out.

Another way to improve your chances of success in sabotaging the septic system is to dump a pound or so of dry yeast into the tank. The yeast will grow at an alarming rate, giving off gases that will back up in the pipes and ultimately waft through your target's home like a breath of . . .

HOUSE OF HORRORS

If you've ever rented accommodation, you'll know exactly what horrors landlords are able to let out to desperate tenants. Blue velour couches and flame-coloured nylon shag-pile carpets are usually the least of your worries—it's the wonky heating, dodgy pipes, and insect infestation that can make a tenant's life truly unbearable. If you've suffered at the hands of a lax landlord and are about to leave his life for good, why not give him a little leaving present in the form of an extended family of six-legged tenants?

Buy a few bags of sugar, then go to the fuse box and turn off the electricity supply. Unscrew the light-switch plates and, using a small funnel, pour a good amount of sugar into each wall cavity. If you've already got a cockroach infestation problem, this should help them multiply to plague proportions, but you can make sure by buying a supply of live cock-roaches (available as pet food from specialist suppli-ers—look at the classified ads in magazines for fish and reptile owners) and funnelling them through the hole after you've dumped the sugar down. Now screw the switch plates back in place and turn the power back on.

EXTERMINATE THEM

Another way of causing your landlord some stick with insects is to send off a bogus letter to the neighbours from either the Terminator Pest Control Company or a fictitious officer at the health department of the local council. Have the letter say something to the effect that you are writing to advise them that number 111 (your former address) has been found to be infested with the rapacious Venezuelan cockroach/wasp/ant. Go into detail about the damage they can cause or the diseases they can carry and say that it is vital the council be notified if the infestation spreads. Describe the insect in some detail—but make sure that what you describe is your standard cockroach, wasp, or ant.

You can make this ploy seem more realistic by posting an appropriate warning notice on the fence or gate. Even if the neighbours confront your ex-landlord and he denies having an infestation problem, your neighbours are unlikely to believe him. Naturally, this ploy would work with any target, so really let your imagination rip. Advise your target's neighbours to avoid socialising with him, tell them to place an antiseptic footbath outside their front door and to change it on a daily basis, advise them to cross the street rather than walk past the infected premises, and add a sentence to say that observing these practices will avoid the need for total evacuation and decontamination of the street.

Even if your target was Mr/Mrs Unpopular before your smear campaign, you can guarantee he or she will start to wonder exactly what's bugging the neighbours.

CLUCK OFF

If the idea of insects makes you squirm, cause a real stink for your landlord by dropping chicken legs down the wiring holes just before you leave. The smell won't become really foul for a couple of days. Dead mice and fish heads add a new meaning to aromatherapy, too.

OCEANS OF IDEAS

Even better than the above is the brilliant idea one wonderfully vengeful woman had to get back at her ex-lover. Having packed her bags to leave the love nest, she decided to get out her sewing kit and do a few minor alterations to the curtains. She carefully unpicked the lining and replaced the weights in the hems with several pounds of peeled prawns before neatly resewing the hems.

As you can imagine, after a couple of days the prawns were higher than high, but the ex-lover was utterly baffled as to the source of the sickening stench. Eventually, of course, he found out what she'd done, but by then the curtains were ruined and his home reeked.

If you're not as handy with a needle and thread as our heroine, try filling hollow curtain rods with a pound or two of prawns, lay them along the picture rail if your target's home has a seldom-dusted one, or express your frustration by slipping a few crustaceans into the underside of removable sofa cushion covers.

A REAL TURN-OFF

If you merely want to take the light out of his life, buy a supply of fishing sinkers and, before you leave, unscrew the switch plates. Make absolutely sure the power is turned off at the mains, then cut the wires leading to the switches. Attach the sinkers to the wires and let them fall to the floor inside the wall. Rescrew the plates—use superglue for added effect if you like—and leave. Your landlord will need more than a spark of ingenuity to sort that one out.

Less obvious but just as effective is changing the rating of the fuse wire in the fuse box. With the electricity turned off, substitute a wire of a much lower rating, so that that the fuse will blow as soon as the power is turned back on. Make sure you thoughtfully leave a supply of spare substitute wire wrapped around a card for the normal rating in the fuse box, so that when the landlord tries to rectify the problem, the same thing will happen again. A good way to put your landlord on a short fuse.

On the subject of wiring, if you're sure you can get away without having to foot the bill, sabotage electrical appliances like the fridge, cooker, and kettle by cutting the flex off at the base. Leave the severed flex in place and plugged in so the problem isn't immediately obvious.

Another way to cause trouble is to tamper with the electricity or gas meter—but beware, there are big penalties if you are caught. Perhaps the best thing would be to find out where your landlord lives and to have a go at his meter. At the very least, he'll have some explaining to do.

CUT IT OUT

Of course, why should you have to do all the work when you can get someone else to do it for you—and an expert, at that? With a little research, it's an easy matter to get your target's electricity, water, or telephone cut off (unfortunately, unless you can manage to intercept your target's gas bills so that he or she is cut off for nonpayment, you'll find it rather tricky to interrupt the gas supply).

Arrange to have each utility cut off seemingly at random, or go for the triple whammy and take out all four at once for maximum inconvenience.

To get the electricity disconnected, you'll need to know the name the account is in if there is more than one person living at your target's address and the account number (you might be able to bluff this one if you can rattle off the address and other relevant details). You'll also have to tell the day you want the electricity cut off. They'll need about a week's notice and, unfortunately, access to your target's house to give a final meter reading, so you'll have to devise a way of working round this obstacle—perhaps ensuring that you or someone else turns up at the same time as the meter reader to distract your target's attention (she'll probably think it's just the usual meter reading anyway).

For the telephone, phone 150 and say you want to have "your" phone disconnected. You'll have to quote the target's name and account number (once again, you might just be able to bluff this one) and nominate the date you want the line disconnected. It pays to know a few other details (address, phone number, etc.), too.

To get the water disconnected, check with your target's local water supplier for details, but you'll probably have to put the request in writing, stating the target's address, account number, and the date you want the water cut off. There will probably be a disconnection fee of around £30, so include a postal order for the appropriate amount. The deed will be done from the outside mains, so your target won't know what's hit him—but you can be sure it won't be the invigorating blast of his morning shower.

CHILLING OUT

Back on the subject of fuses, here's another way to make your deep-freeze-owning target blow his. You'll need a blown fuse and, if possible, the leeway provided by your target's being away for a few days. Unplug the freezer and leave the door or lid open for as long as possible to speed the defrosting process. Now, open the plug and substitute the blown fuse for the good one. Plug the freezer back in and turn it on. It won't work because of the blown fuse. When your target returns, his freezer will be well and truly defrosted, and anything inside it will have to be thrown out. Best of all, there's nothing to indicate that the blown fuse didn't happen all of its own accord. Such a nice way to thaw the icy relations between you.

IN HOT WATER

If you move out in the summer, why not leave a little time-delay surprise for your landlord? Use a radiator key to loosen the bleed points on the central heating radiators, then make sure you take it with you or throw it out when you finally leave. With the first cold spell, your little hex will leave your landlord having to deal with floods of complaints from his irate tenants.

Alternatively, try scoring the radiator pipes till

you're almost—but not quite—through. Paint over the cutting lines if necessary to disguise the damage. Come winter, the pipes will be put through expansion as the hot water runs through them and contraction when the heating goes off, a process that will eventually weaken them along the score marks till they leak, once again leaving your landlord swimming in it.

While you're engaged in plumbing the depths of the plumbing, why not paint a liberal coating of hydrochloric acid on the lead seal of the water pipes? That should leave the pipes—and your landlord—fit to burst.

Another way to turn your whine into water is to target your landlord's home. Slip a length of hose through the letter-box in the door and use a funnel to pour whatever substance you like through it and into his home.

An alternative would be to release the contents of a fire extinguisher through the letter-box, or a can or five of quick-drying expanding insulation foam. If there's a convenient garden tap and hosepipe nearby, so much the better. Slip the nozzle through the door, turn the tap on and give it a burst, then replace everything as it was. Or, if you really want to put a damper on your target, leave it running.

FLOOR THEM

Aside from the water damage the above stunt will cause, you'll also have the satisfaction of knowing that damp carpet, especially if it's an old one, will smell awful. But it will also be irreparably damaged if mould just happens to grow on it after it's been soaked.

Time your indoor watering scam for when your target is going to be away for an few days and have ready a few pieces of mouldy bread. (Lightly dampen a few slices of fresh bread—use a brand that doesn't list mould inhibitors on the wrapping —expose them to the air for a couple of hours, then seal them in a plastic bag and leave in a warmish dark place. Unless you live in a sterile environment, you should have a nice crop of pink, black, and green mould in no time at all.) Dampen your target's carpet thoroughly with water and leave the mouldy bread on top. If it's warm enough, the mould should take hold and you'll leave your target with an interesting new colour scheme on his carpet.

Can't be bothered to go to all that trouble? Well, forget the water and the mould and just rake up a carrier bag full of pine needles and dump them through the letter-box. They're hell to get out of carpet, especially if it's shag-pile.

SEEDS OF DISCORD

Another way to bring a bit of greenery into your target's life is to sow the dampened carpet thickly with mustard and cress seed. A couple of days should be all that's needed for these hardy salad seeds to sprout and take hold, turning her floor covering into an attractive carpet of living greenery that will be next to impossible to get rid of once it's taken root.

THE WRITING'S ON THE FLOOR

Still on the subject of carpets, try using a syringe filled with thick bleach to spell an appropriate message on your target's carpet. The bleach will strip the dye out of the fibres, leaving your target with an indelible reminder of how someone really feels about him.

Or you could simply let your target spoil the carpet himself. Substitute bleach for his carpet shampoo, and watch the colour drain out of his face—and carpet—next time he has a cleaning spree.

BENCH MARK POSITION

Ever noticed how the labels on limescale remover and glass cleaning solution warn you to keep the product away from marble? There's a very good reason: they eat into it and etch the smooth surface. So imagine how awful—and expensive—it would be if some of the stuff came into contact with your target's lovely marble coffee table, or her prized marble kitchen work tops, especially if when it was spilled it happened to spell an unfortunate word or message? Well, at least she could legitimately say, "Come up and see my etchings".

KEYED UP

As revealed in more detail in the chapter on cars, locks offer a multitude of opportunities to cause your target grief. Superglue them up or jam a spare key in and then hacksaw the end off. Both these ploys have the added bonus that you don't even have to gain access to your target's home—you can simply do it from the outside, and it works whether your target is at home or out.

Another neat way to keep your target in—or out—is to fit a sturdy hasp and keeper to the door and door frame. Slap a padlock on the new fixture and throw away the key.

Make more trouble for your target by changing any padlocks on, for example, his bicycle. Make sure you use identical models if you really want to drive him round the bend.

HANDLE WITH CARE

While you're by the door, why not saw off the doorknob or handle? Refix it with a dab or two of epoxy so that it looks normal, but don't add too much glue. The idea is that, if not on the first use, then certainly on the second or third, the handle will simply come off in your target's hand, leaving him knobbled, so to speak.

SOFT OPTION

An alternative to the old steaming-dog-turd-through-the-letter-box trick is to get your doggy mess and wrap it loosely in a single sheet of newspaper. Now, set light to the newspaper, dump the dump on the doorstep, ring the bell, and run. The aim is to get your target to the door to see the blaze, which, hopefully, he will then attempt to stamp out. Squelch!

CHOKE ON IT

If your target likes nothing more in winter that a blazing log fire and you can gain access to his roof, why not try the old smoke cure? Secure a couple of extra-strong bin liners over the chimney (or a paving slab, piece of metal, or even a rubbish bin lid) and wait for your target to light up. It shouldn't take more than 20 minutes for him to be smoked out—but it will take a lot longer than that for the campfire smell to be aired out of his home.

If you want to boost the wood smoke odour into something truly vile, try adding some sulphur to the logs in the grate before you wrap up the chimney. When burned, the sulphur will smell overpoweringly of rotten eggs.

BAD BLOOD

Ask a helpful butcher for a bucket of pig's blood (mention how fond you are of home-made black pudding if you want to avoid suspicion). Now freeze it in ice-cream containers. Pack it in ice cubes when you're ready to use it, then transport it to your target's home. Leave your block of blood in a drawer, filing cabinet, or cupboard and imagine his terror when he discovers the pool of congealing blood. In a similar vein, freeze the blood in ice-cube-size portions and leave them all over the house in a gory trail (stick a couple in the shower head for a *Psycho*-style effect), or unscrew one of the switch plates and dump the lot through the hole into the wall cavity and wait for it to start to seep through the wall (make sure the wall isn't dry-lined, though, or your efforts will go to waste). Bloodcurdling, eh?

An alternative would be to freak out the downstairs neighbours. Place the block of blood either under the bed where it won't be seen or, if you can, lever up a couple of floorboards and place the block in the space between the downstairs ceiling and your target's floor. As the blood melts, it should seep through the ceiling, leaving an awful, terrifying stain and possibly dripping in a convincingly nightmarish way. Imagine how difficult it's going to be for your target to convince the police—and the neighbours—that he has no idea how the blood got there.

TURN OVER A NEW LEAF

Pot plants can be a good way to get to the root of the problem if your target is one of the green-fingered variety. Try watering her pride and joy with an extremely concentrated salt solution, or denaturing nature by adding neat food colouring to the soil for an alarming variegated look.

ONE FOR THE RECORD

Remember LPs—those round bits of vinyl that used to give people hours of listening pleasure? Well, some Luddites still have them, and some of them are very valuable indeed, if only in terms of sentimental value to their owners. If your target is one of these people, help her do the time warp again by shoving her entire collection—minus the sleeves, which should remain tidily in place on her shelve—in the oven. Set it for 35 minutes at 350°F, at the end of which time the stack should be meltingly tender. Who said revenge was a dish best served cold?

TANKED UP

If you live in a house that's been divided into flats and there's something festering between you and one of the other flat owners or tenants, try sabotaging his cold-water storage tank with something equally putrid. Lob a dead mouse or rat into it—after all, who's to say it couldn't have fallen in there accidentally—or simply pee in it.

With a bit more planning, you could really make him squirm. Get a couple of bags of live water fleas from an aquarium supplier (they're used for tropical fish food) and pour them into the tank. Next time your target takes a bath, he'll find himself sharing it with a few thousand unwelcome guests.

Another way to freak your target out is to add a few packets of deep red dye to the water tank. Experiment with dilutions at home till you get an approximation of blood red so that you can turn shower time into a real bloodbath.

STROKE OF GENIUS

Awful as it is to deface art, sometimes it's the only way to get even—but we're not suggesting out-and-out vandalism. Subtlety is the name of the game. Take that exquisite eighteenth-century portrait in your target's hall—who would notice if, among the jewels at her wrist, a masterfully executed digital watch was to appear? Get the picture?

STRANGE BEDFELLOWS

Those of you who have ever been subjected to boarding school will know all about short-sheeting and apple pies at the bottom of the bed. Why not brighten up your target's nights with something a little more lively?

Try slipping a mouse or rat into the duvet cover, or shoveling a pound of bait maggots, worms, or live cockroaches into the foot of the bed (make sure the sheets—and your target's sleeping partners—are tucked in nice and tightly. That should give him bad dreams for some time to come—and wake him up the fact that he's done something to deserve it.

MAKE YOUR MARK

For the final word in home-made revenge, head for your target's library. So, he's one of those posers who has shelves full of the latest controversial books—all unread.

Why not encourage him to at least open some of his purchases by leaving him a few tasteful bookmarks—in the form of thinly sliced hard cheese, salami, or prosciutto? A nice way to bring one chapter of your life to a satisfactory conclusion.

Bureaucracy

*B*ureaucracy is everywhere. It's a national disease. No, it's an international disease, and all areas of our lives, from our schools to our political decisions, are shaped by the pen-pushing jobsworths. Bureaucracy is, ultimately, unbeatable. However you vote (or even if you don't) you're stuck with the rules of the bureaucrats. You can, however, score minor victories, whether it's inducing paranoia in a credit-card company, pissing off a politician, or just treating Big Brother like a member of your own family and setting him on all your worst enemies . . .

GOVERNMENT DEPARTMENTS
FLY THE FLAG

Prove to the world what a patriotic soul your target is by raising the colours on the roof of his or her home . . . the colours of another country, that is. Select a regime that is most likely to go down badly with the neighbours, and time it to coincide with some particularly evil deed perpetrated by the nation in question. Iranian and Iraqi flags are always likely to cause tension, especially around Aldershot and other military bases. Similarly patriotic car pennants and stickers are also an excellent idea, especially if you position them at the back of the car, where your target may not notice them for days. Phone the relevant embassies and consulates for flag stockists. You could even drop them a line in your target's name, telling them what an admirer you are. Be sure to choose a regime your target hates intensely.

In fact, registering your enemy with a variety of extremist political groups can be fun because it gets him unwelcome attention from two directions—the organisation he has unwittingly "joined" and the police. Think about it. If banks and supermarkets are now allowed to keep files on their employees' sex lives, don't you think the police have ways of monitoring the membership of any potentially antisocial groups?

The arrival of *glasnost* and *perestroika* may have done away with the Russians as the favourite source of Western paranoia, but you can still make your target feel like James Bond by making him the recipient of coded messages from international powers.

If your target works for the police, security services, or is in the army, acquire some headed notepaper from the offices of a potentially hostile power—a bland enquiry to the consulate about visa requirements will furnish you with this. Cover the words with a sheet of plain white paper and photocopy several times to produce virgin sheets of headed paper. If you can get to a good-quality colour photocopier, so much the better. Then send a bizarre cryptic coded letter to your target at work—for example, "The sun is rising in the Malvinas" on headed paper from the Argentinian embassy, or just "Sunday, 1 P.M., Rushdie" from the "Iranians". With luck, somebody else will open your target's post and will be very intrigued indeed.

MOONLIGHTING BECOMES YOU

If your enemy is on the dole, call the DHSS and tell them he's making £300 a week tax-free, painting and decorating. So many people moonlight that your man may well be caught red-handed. Even if he's clean, he'll have to answer lots of very nosy questions and will probably be watched very carefully in the future.

Should your target be gainfully employed, make it appear that his gains are fuller than he says. Make an anonymous call to the Inland Revenue explaining that Mr Target has been boasting at work about how he dodges taxes he should be paying from his free-lance business on the side. If pressed to give your name, give that of your second-worst enemy.

You can then give your target a call and tell him that you are from the Inland Revenue and are doing an investigation into his records from five years ago. Choose a Friday (this will give him the whole week-end to think about it), and say that there appear to be some inconsistencies, but insist that you cannot be drawn into details on the phone. Ask to see him, with all his paperwork, at 9 A.M. Monday, and give him the actual address of the local IR offices.

YOU'RE NICKED

Also on these lines, word reached us about an individual who was selling electrical goods that had fallen off the back of the proverbial lorry—and worked as if they had, too. One local electrical goods salesman was particularly fed up because this dodgy customer would send potential customers into his shop to ask questions and find out what they wanted and then have them come back to him to place their orders. The shop owner got his revenge by printing up a fake letterhead and organised an advert in the local paper for his bogus competitor. On the fake letterhead, he wrote to the Inland Revenue and the VAT man asking for a visit as he needed to straighten out his finances before the end of the tax year and was concerned that a visit might be overdue.

When the Revenue contacted his competitor, he tried to pass it off as a hoax, but as he was "advertising" in the local paper, nobody believed him. It turned out he did owe quite a lot of tax and VAT, plus, the police put him under a great deal of pressure to be more specific about his suppliers. He went out of business shortly afterward.

WET DREAM

Tired of one of the big, inefficient publicly owned monopolies that the government has recently turned into big, inefficient, privately owned monopolies (now *there's* progress)? Take, for example, the water authority—all of them. Few people have noticed great improvements in the service. In fact, we're always hearing about how filthy the stuff is, and yet, prices are rumoured to be going up by as much as 50 per cent over the next few years.

It's time somebody spoke out—so why not you, on your local water authority's behalf? Give yourself a new name and an official-sounding title, such as Public Relations Associate for the Rutshire Water Board. And get yourself an "office" (see the Yellow Pages for telephone message companies that will answer your calls personally, as though you had an office there). Then contact small local radio stations offering yourself as a guest to "talk through" the latest ideas on water conservation. Give them your card (cheaply acquired from one of those anonymous machines at major railway stations) and encourage them to call you at your office (where they'll only ever be able to leave a message but will think they've just missed you).

Most small radio stations are desperate for guests, so it shouldn't be long before somebody has a gap to fill and takes up your kind offer. You will, of course, seem quite sane beforehand, but as soon as you go on air, your tone will change. Here are some of the policies you might like to espouse in the name of your local water board:

- *An immediate ban on all aquariums and noncactus ornamental plants, both inside and outside all public and private places.*
- *All human and pet corpses to be completely dehydrated in company factories to remove all usable water before burial and cremation.*

- *In one month's time, all fresh water will be shut off to private homes two days a week and to industry three days a week unless those concerned take out a special "Private Water Care Plan", which will ensure round-the-clock cover.*
- *Members of the public will be encouraged to buy filters to purify washing machine and bath water to be recycled for drinking purposes.*
- *Introduction of mandatory metering on the number of times toilets may be flushed daily.*

If that doesn't cause some damp patches at the local water authority, nothing will.

I'M STILL WAITING

There are some extremely rude bureaucrats who refuse to answer their calls and assume they are more important than the people they are supposed to be serving.

If you have had one too many of your calls unanswered, here's the drill.: Say to the person on the other end of the line, "I didn't want to have to bring (full name of chief executive) into this little matter. I thought your (name of faceless bureaucrat) could take care of it him/herself, but obviously that's not the case. Well, I'm calling (first name of chief executive) to invite him over to lunch soon, so I suppose I'll have to discuss this matter with him then."

Most faceless bureaucrats are too wimpish to take a chance over something like this, and they'll be on that phone, full of apologies.

COURTROOM DRAMA

If your target is a married man who has, or has had, girlfriends on the side, why not sue him for palimony? Mock up a realistic-looking solicitor's letterhead and drop him a line to the effect that his ex will see him in court. Never mind that they never actually lived together. Throw in that his ex alleges that he used to beat her and that this evidence is corroborated by hospitals she visited late at night on evenings when witnesses saw them together. Perhaps your philanderer will be so scared about his wife finding out that he'll come clean to her—and that will be the start of his real problems, because with luck, *she'll* take *him* to the cleaners.

BUGGER ABOUT

Paranoid targets are easy prey. Drop a business card belonging to a "private investigator" on their front lawn or drive for your target to find. This is just the start. There are several shops that specialise in surveillance equipment (see "Private Eye" chapter) and, with their help you can convince your target he is being spied on.

Get a friend to follow your target in an obvious way, making notes in a book. When spotted, your friend should hold the target's gaze for a moment before running off as quickly as possible. Add to the paranoia by leaving a cheap recording device by your target's vehicle or home. It should look as though it has been dropped by someone who was disturbed and had to get away in a hurry.

BANKERS

There are few people who have not, at one time or another, been badly treated by a bank. Petty, humourless and, above all, powerful—after all, they have your money—they are, nevertheless vulnerable to the able avenger. Dropping stink bombs in the foyer, supergluing door locks or gluing pens to the desks in the foyer, and feeding cash-card machines superglue-covered cards all leave banks feeling short-changed.

CHANGE FOR THE WORSE

The truly brave might feel better after making a particularly rude cashier feel stupid. Burst into the bank lobby one busy afternoon wearing a ski mask and gloves and rush up to the counter in an extremely aggressive fashion. Thrust a note to the cashier while glaring menacingly at customers and other employees. The note should read, "Please can you change this £20 note for me? I have a taxi waiting."

IN SAFE HANDS

Make the bank splash out for a change. Dress smartly and wait, with a large, businesslike bag, by the bank's night safe. When a night safe depositor arrives, explain you have forgotten your night safe key/access number, that you have the day's takings in the bag (show him the bag), and that you wouldn't feel safe if you had to take it home. Could he open the safe and let you deposit the bag? Usually the answer is yes, as few people suspect individuals who are trying to make a deposit. In the bag is a time-delay smoke bomb. When it goes off it will trigger the alarm and sprinkler system, causing hundreds of pounds worth of damage. Never before will smoking have been so bad for your bank manager's health.

Using a disguise or a friend from a different area, open a safe-deposit box at the target branch. The classic trick is to deposit a dead fish and never return. The smell will, of course, be foul and the management won't know which box it's coming from. If you can, put some superglue on the bottom of the box to make the contents that much harder to remove and, if you're left alone down there at all, put some superglue into the locks of other boxes while you're at it.

DIRTY MONEY

As the banks are always telling us, we have to learn to make our money work for us. So why not write your target's personal details on every piece of paper money you get hold of? List his name, address, home and work telephone numbers, national insurance number, and credit card numbers on all that lovely cash, and hope the information falls into the wrong hands. A variation on this theme is to use the note as an advertising billboard offering unusual sexual services on your target's behalf —with his or her home and work telephone numbers, of course. People never throw money away, so it'll just stay in circulation until the bank of England takes it out of circulation, and they, too, will probably be very keen to speak to sleazy individuals who are defacing their bills for dubious purposes.

POLITICIANS

The most powerful weapon that can be used against politicians is the ability to make them look stupid. You could be forgiven for thinking that this is a relatively easy task, but these men and women tend to surround themselves with lackeys whose sole purpose in life is to prevent them from saying or doing something that might show them in a less-than-perfect light.

In time-honoured tradition, you could turn up wherever Public Enemy No. 1 is due to appear and attempt to raise an insulting—or just accurate—placard behind him as he is being interviewed on live TV, or dress up in uniformlike garb and approach the target, confidently offering to take his coat. The impression is that you are going to hang it up for him, but what you actually do with it is up to you. Perhaps someone down at Cardboard City could use it?

POLITICALLY INCORRECT

At election time, it's important your target gets his message across to the masses, so why no help him out? Using your trusty home computer or trusted printer friend, print out a mass of leaflets detailing your candidate's "policies". Perhaps your Tory candidate would like to legalise not just marijuana, but ecstasy, heroin, and cocaine, "because they cost too much to police and only kill off useless members of our society".

Or maybe your target is a Labour MP. How about revealing his private member's bill to get the country's police forces sponsored by big business—the Sainsbury's Flying Squad, Toys 'R' Us Special Branch, etc.? The only problem with this is that it could back-fire and the local idiots might actually vote for it.

You might also volunteer your MP for charity work. Acquire some House of Commons-headed notepaper through the usual channels of making a pointless enquiry and then photocopy the whited-out sheet. Write to a hospital saying that the MP will be in the area and wishes to visit the children's ward of the hospital in two days' time. Then phone, before the letter arrives, identifying yourself as the MP's secretary and telling them about the letter. Explain that you and the MP will be out of the office all day for the next few days, but you will phone again to reconfirm. The hospital press officer will then set the PR wheels in motion, and the local press—and maybe even TV, depending on the importance of your target—will be there. People will be very annoyed when he simply fails to show up, and he'll be feeling a bit sick about all the adverse publicity, too.

THE POLICE

Naturally, the police are an important part of many revenge scenarios. Anonymously reporting your target's involvement in a cross-section of crimes, from car theft to drug dealing to flashing, can be a highly rewarding pastime. However, it's even better if you can get your target to "waste police time" by reporting crimes that never were.

Mannequin Piss-take

Take, for example, the simulated murder. You'll need a store dummy, weighted down with sand and dressed in realistic clothing. If you can be recognised by your target, get someone else to "struggle" with the dummy in full view of your target before pushing the dummy off a bridge or out of a window (make sure it falls somewhere where it can't easily be reached—like onto the roof of another, smaller building). Your law-abiding target will hopefully call the old Bill, who will then waste precious time rescuing a dummy.

Another idea is to arrange the "suicide" of a dummy, partially weighting it, dressing it, and dropping it into a river. Your "dead" dummy should have a note about his or her person identifying him or herself as your target and explaining that she/he couldn't go on with the pressure of all the extramarital affairs (many of which involved young children) and the guilt of recent illegal business deals. Phone the police, telling them you've found a dead body in such-and-such a place, but refusing to give your details because you "don't want to get involved". Then phone the local radio station with details about this bizarre hoax, where it is, what the note says, and so on. With luck it'll make the local news.

Getting back at a policeman is harder, but getting him to witness you "stealing" something—a garden ornament or park bench—which actually turns out to belong to you (you will, of course, have receipts to prove it) will go some way to making the boy in blue go very red indeed.

MAIL-ORDER AND
CREDIT-CARD COMPANIES

If you can get access to an empty house, you have all the tools you need to wreak profitable revenge on the mail-order book or record companies whose irritating advertisements drop out of every magazine in the country. Fill in the form, giving the empty house as your address and using a false name, and select best-selling books or chart albums—choose items that are sold everywhere. When the goodies arrive, take them to a large shop and explain that they were presents and that you would like to change them. You probably won't be able to get "your" money back, even if you can find a receipt of the appropriate value, but the selection will be better at the shop, and you can pick things you really want.

Make your next order large (this is the last one you'll be able to make before they start chasing the money) and you'll finally appreciate all the benefits of home shopping they keep telling you about. Actually, you don't have to limit yourself to books and records. While travelling in Southeast Asia, I met a woman who had financed her trip to Borneo by ordering electrical goods from big mail-order catalogue firms. In her case, there was no trouble getting credit because she used her real name and address. It was just that she was never planning to come back.

CREDIT WHERE IT'S DUE

If you really hate your credit-card company but feel powerless to move it in any way at all, here's one way you can pay it back in a sense other than the purely financial. It hurts because it's unexpected: it's a letter from someone thanking the company for its excellent service. Here's how it goes:

Dear (Chairman of the board),

This is the tenth anniversary of my association with Barclaycard/Access/American Express, and I would like to thank you personally for your corporation's unflagging generosity.

It started, I suppose, with my credit-card application, which was promptly denied for reasons I've long since forgotten. Then, strangely, a card from your company bearing my name followed shortly thereafter.

I began to use the new card, assuming that your applications department had made an error in rejecting my application. I might add that I used the card exclusively, as I had no other credit card. Two, three, four months passed, and it occurred to me that I had received no bill. Although I kept few receipts, I calculated my purchases to be well over 100 pounds. As the expiry date on my card approached, I was certain the computer accounting error would be revealed, a mammoth bill sent and no replacement card issued.

The years have gone by now, as I've said, ten in all, and as regular as clockwork a new plastic card arrives just in time to replace the old one—but never an invoice. After all these years I have grown confident that my name and number are locked, eternally silent, in a minuscule electrical impulse somewhere in some computer's faulty diode or senile memory bank.

Or, it may be that I have a secret friend in your company itself—someone who is helping me, unbeknownst to me. I wonder how many other people are being "helped" in this way and have chosen not to write to you?

Unable to repay you now, even if I were billed, I can only send you this note of thanks.

Yours sincerely,

A Very Satisfied Customer

SCHOOLS

Most people of school age are inventive enough when it comes to classroom disruption, but here are a few ideas on how fight back against tedious teachers and blackboard bores:

Strike Back

Make a small hollow in the tip of a piece of chalk and fill it with a match head. Glue back some of the displaced chalk powder to cover it, but leave the very top exposed. As soon as that piece of chalk hits the blackboard, your teacher will see the light.

Draw or paste something obscene on pull-down maps and screens. Institute massive searches for "lost" contact lenses during particularly dull assemblies or lessons.

When you have undisturbed access to the classroom at the end of the day, varnish the blackboard using a can of artist's spray varnish. This will give the appearance of a freshly wiped blackboard—until the teacher attempts the impossible task of writing on it. Alternatively, if your school uses the more modern white boards with magic markers, spray on your varnish when the board is covered in writing after a lesson, and it will be impossible to remove. You could even leave a message of your own before spraying.

Free captured animals and insects being held prisoner in the biology labs.

Demand to see your own school records—everybody has the right to see records relating to him or her and to take issue with these records if he or she sees fit.

Acquire school-headed paper by blanking out and photocopying any letter the school has sent to your home. Then put up some official notices of your own around school regarding new rules.

Pupil Power
Targeting a school bully or idle creep who hasn't been caught up with yet? Come report time, prepare a little progress report of your own. Take one of your own old school report sheets and photocopy it. Then Tippex out the teachers' marks and

comments and photocopy again. This will leave you with a pristine report sheet. Next, type in the comments and marks you think your target actually deserves. Avoid being too abusive; stick to the arch, sarcastic, and generally nasty teacher style, as this is more likely to be believed. Send it out about a week before the genuine ones go out, and wait for the reaction.

If your target is not a pupil but a parent, call him just after school hours and say you are the head teacher and you need to speak to him urgently regarding a disciplinary matter. Arrange to meet him or her at 8 o'clock the following morning.

Teacher's Pest

Finally, this one's for teachers. Sick of trying to educate some poisonous little shit who is rude, disruptive, violent, and impossible to control? As you will never be able to control him through any official channels—the law won't even let the police do that—give him a few sobering moments in the privacy of his own home.

Next time the school nurse comes round to give the kids their immunisation jabs, get a friend to call the parents a few days later, identifying him or herself as a doctor at the council's schools clinic. Explain that while they were giving the kids their jabs, they took a blood sample to check for anaemia and hepatitis and have discovered in the course of testing that their son has syphilis (herpes, AIDS, whatever). Explain that as this is such a sensitive condition, the council thinks it best that they, the parents, inform the child in order to prevent further spread of the disease through intercourse, and that they should, without delay, make an appointment for their son to see their GP for a check-up and the appropriate medication.

Cars

An Englishman's home may well be his castle, but it's more often his car that's his pride and joy—making it a prime target for those with vengeance on their minds. One of the best ways to drive your point home is to make sure your target won't be driving anywhere—except the garage —and experienced avengers know that this can be arranged in almost as many ways as there are moving parts in an engine.

So, with that gleaming penis substitute firmly in your sights, it simply remains for you to chose an appropriate way to hit your target where it hurts— below the belt. Anything is possible, from temporary disfigurement to terminal shafting, and, if it's done skillfully enough, you'll have the satisfaction of leaving your target impotent with rage.

FUEL FOR THOUGHT

Any number of substances can be added either to

a car's fuel tank or crankcase as vehicles for revenge. Some of them you'll have to hand already; others will necessitate a trip to your nearest DIY or car accessories store.

Getting to the petrol tank might be difficult if you don't have keys, but even if you have to lever open the cover to get at the cap, your target will be so grateful to find the fuel hasn't been siphoned out that he'll never consider that something altogether nastier might have happened.

Starting with the petrol tank, shellac varnish thinner is always a good bet. It won't do any lasting damage, and it's readily available from hardware shops and DIY centres. You'll need about a gallon to do the job properly. The substance works by gathering up all the water in the fuel trap. As it goes through to the carburettor, so does the water, making the engine cough and splutter like an emphysema victim. It's guaranteed to make your target think he's got big carburettor problems, but the beauty of it is that by the time he gets to his mechanic, the culprit will have disappeared in a puff of smoke out through the tailpipe. Repeat this at intervals, and not only will your target think he's driving a lemon, but his mechanic will think he's got a paranoid time-waster on his hands.

No shellac thinner? Well, water is always a good standby. Heavier than fuel, it will sink to the bottom of the tank and be taken up by the fuel line as soon as the car gets going. Add enough and you'll bring the car to a wheezing, shuddering halt.

Another matchless way to get your target's car coughing like a 60-a-day smoker is to introduce it to the evil weed. Simply slit open a cigar and slip it into the petrol tank. It will take a little while for the tobacco to shred finely enough to start clogging the fuel line, but, once it does, your target will have a real engine health hazard on his hands. Another plus point is that simply getting the fuel line cleared won't extinguish the problem. Any tobacco remaining in the tank will cause the problem again and again until your smouldering target finally realises he'll have to cough up to get the fuel tank cleaned out.

Sugar brings new meaning to the term "sweet revenge". As it combusts, it turns to carbon, leaving a lovely residue in the cylinders and a car that won't be going anywhere in a hurry. Use icing sugar for best results.

Old-fashioned mothballs work even better because they dissolve completely in petrol, leaving no visible evidence and getting to work faster to ensure that your target certainly won't. And melted candle wax, by all accounts, is another good way to get on someone's wick.

If you've really got an axe to grind, why stop there? Go for abrasive action by adding very fine metal filings or sand, or, even better, Carborundum, which you can get from ironmongers or hobby shops selling polishing materials for rock collectors. Powder is best, but you might have to settle for paste. A dollop or so in the petrol tank should be enough to make the engine sound really rough.

Another way to have your target eat his heart out is to add battery acid to the fuel. In addition to paralyzing the car, you'll have the added satisfaction of knowing it's doing a great job of corroding the guts out of it.

If your target's a speed freak and always banging on about how fast his car is, why not help him break his own record? Add some model aeroplane fuel, a volatile mix of methanol and nitromethane, and watch him take off.

For those targets with diesel engines, revenge is astonishingly easy. Give the nuts holding the lines to the injectors a one-eighth twist to loosen them. Do it to alternate cylinders, or all down one side. The idea is to start a small leak, and you can be sure that, with the fuel compressed to 3,000 psi once the engine is started, that small leak will soon become a very big one.

OIL IN A GOOD CAUSE

If doctoring the oil appeals more, you could try adding linseed oil. Normally used for oiling cricket bats and leather, you can get it from most sport stores and saddleries. A tin should be enough to get things moving—or, rather, stop them moving. Unlike engine oil, as linseed oil oxidises, it dries out, so instead of lubricating the moving parts, it binds them right up.

Alternatively, drain the oil, replace the plug, then fill the crankcase with water. This'll do more damage then simply draining the oil, because the water will stop the oil warning light from coming on, leaving your target in blissful ignorance until the engine seizes.

Carborundum, sand, or any other abrasive will do

a nice job of destroying piston rings and bearings, too, but for truly spectacular results, the prime additive has to be styrene. A colourless, oily liquid and one of the two chemicals that are mixed to form fibreglass, styrene also has a diabolical effect on oil, serving to break it down completely. It's readily available from boatyard chandlers, and you'll need about a pint to do the job properly. Your target's car will run about 100 miles before the effects become apparent and his expensive engine is turned into a piece of worthless scrap metal.

If your target drives an automatic, it makes sense to get him where it will hurt his hip-pocket nerve the most—the transmission. A pint or so of battery acid mixed in with the transmission fluid will wreck it nicely and throw your target's driving plans into reverse.

BALLS IT UP

Why not get straight to the heart of the matter? Remove a couple of spark-plugs, drop a few small ball bearings into the cylinders, then replace the plugs. The results are reassuringly expensive to repair.

RUNAWAY SUCCESS

A very, very small amount of solvent dropped into the master cylinder of the brake system will slowly eat away all rubber parts, causing a gradual, expensive, and totally unstoppable breakdown of the brakes. Far more subtle than cutting the brake cables.

DELIVER A CRUSHING BLOW

This tactic is in the classic "you've been framed" mould. It takes a bit of planning, but it's great if you want to see your target totally crushed. First, you'll need to find out whether there is a way of moving your target's car. It doesn't have to be very far; around the corner or even just a little way up the road will do. Having carried out your feasibility study, make a trip to a car breaker's and select a newly crushed car (too much rust will give the game away), preferably a similar model, and, naturally, in the same colour as your target's pride and joy. Buy it and arrange to have it transported to your target's normal parking spot to coincide with your moving his car. Try to make sure you're around to see the reaction.

A variation on this trick is to make your target think his dream car has gone up in smoke. Get your hands on an uncrushed wreck similar to the target's car and set the scene as above. Pour petrol over it, toss a match, and disappear fast.

FILL 'ER UP

Forget the petrol tank for this one. Get hold of one of the big nonmedical syringes available from hardware and car accessories shops and fill it with a Dead Sea-strength salt solution (salt dissolves better in hot water). Now ease the nozzle under the rubber window seals of your target's car and inject it into the door frame. You'll need to repeat this regularly, but your reward will be those tell-tale rust bumps bubbling up through the target's precious paint work.

Another way to inject a little pain into your target's life is with expanding insulation foam. This amazing product (available from hardware shops and DIY centres) comes in either a single can or a two-can mix and, on contact with air, foams up impressively, then hardens into solid mass. Spray it wherever you like—in the engine compartment, in the boot, or fill up the entire interior with the stuff.

WHAT'S COOKING?

The radiator is another prime target for the serious saboteur. Corrosives like battery acid and salt are the obvious evil additives, but for the culinary-minded, there's plenty of scope for creativity. Why not cook the engine by adding sugar, yeast, and flour to the radiator water? Quick-cooking rice is also guaranteed to bring things to the boil, while plain black pepper—4 tablespoons should be enough—is not to be sneezed at when it comes to finding an effective way of clogging the cooling passages.

While you're in the kitchen, why not whip up a packet of instant pancake batter mix? Pour the gloop over the engine block, preferably after use, while it is still hot, and you're sure to make your target flip.

ONLY CHOKING

While you've got the bonnet up, slip off the air filter and fill the air intake with the powder of your choice: anything from curry powder to powdered fertiliser will do the trick. If you really mean business, though, there's always the old kipper-on-the-engine scam.

Best done in winter when the air intake will be sucking in engine-warmed air to toast your target's tootsies, it simply involves fixing a kipper near the air intake and waiting till your target kicks up a real stink. Chicken legs or fish heads secreted in the boot, under and even inside seats, will ensure there's more than your target's temper running high inside his car, while a pint of milk poured over the carpets will leave a sour atmosphere.

WHAT A COIL

Still under the bonnet, locate the coil and attach a length of wire to the negative terminal (use old, greasy wire so it won't look obvious). Attach the other end of the wire to a suitable earth, and you'll get your target in a fearful coil trying to sort out why his car won't start. This trick will even stump mechanics for a good while.

BRIGHT SPARK

The battery is another sure-fire way to flatten your target. Settle things fast by adding one or two tablets of an antacid like Alka-Seltzer to each well. It won't do much for your target's heartburn, but you're bound to feel a whole lot better. Baking powder does the same thing, neutralising your target in no time, but if you really want to make the sparks fly, simply reverse the battery connections.

MESSAGE IN A BOTTLE

Nail varnish remover has an amazing ability to eat into all kinds of plastic. Devise a neat cardboard stencil with an appropriate message and use it to make your mark on the dashboard or instrument console.

If you can't get into the car, why not invest in a windscreen etching kit? Available from car accessories shops, these kits are normally used to etch identification marks as an antitheft device, but there's no limit to the messages you could leave permanently inscribed for all to see.

EXHAUSTIVE MEASURES

If you don't have keys and therefore easy access to the fuel tank and engine, one of the best ways to disable a car is through the exhaust.

Try shoving a nice, fat banana, cucumber, or potato into the tailpipe—the idea is to create an airtight seal so the carbon monoxide fumes that normally escape are forced back into the fuel system. Properly done, this will result in a build-up of exhaust that will cause the seals on the transmission to disengage, well and truly jiggering the engine.

Plastic filler or the expanding foam mentioned earlier will also do the trick nicely, but make sure you leave enough time for the stuff to dry—and take care to wipe away any tell-tale signs of tampering.

If you want to make things go with a bit more of a bang, try shoving heat-reactive substances up the exhaust: popcorn for a gentle hit; also cylindrical nicad batteries, butane gas lighters, firecrackers; or, if you're feeling really nasty, shotgun shells. A less explosive but equally spectacular way to make your target fume is to insert a plastic phial containing castor oil, WD-40, or plain old engine oil. As the exhaust pipe heats up, the plastic will melt, causing the oil to leak out and burn. The result will be an extremely nonenvironmentally friendly pall of black smoke. Once the oil is burned, the smoke will soon clear, leaving your target relieved but confused. Increase your fun and double his garage bills by repeating the process on a regular basis.

STICKY END

Glue has a multiplicity of uses, and there are so many miracle glues on the market now that you're sure to find just the one you need to fix your target once and for all.

You could start by experimenting with contact adhesives (the sort that set only when something touches them). Try adding some to the female half of the driver's seat belt. While you're inside, why not glue the handset of the car phone to the cradle, or stick the indicator into a permanent left turn? Pick the lock in reverse while you're at it—ram a toothpick into the ignition and then glue it in place.

Glue the exterior locks tight, too—doors, boot, and petrol cap—and for even more effect, force toothpicks into these locks first as well. And don't forget the aerial. A drizzle of thin, fast-drying glue down a retracting aerial well is sure to get a good reception.

Take things a step further and nail your target with a liberal application of liquid nails around the door seals. It should set firm over-night.

Looking for a more subtle way to wipe your target? Use one of the acrylic cements formulated for making model cars and aeroplanes to stick the wipers to the windscreen. If you're lucky, your unsuspecting target will burn the wiper motor out before he realises the fix he's in.

Wipers can also be used to spread trouble: a smear of quick-drying glue along their length and a sprinkle of grit or other abrasive, and your target's view of the world will be jaundiced, to say the least.

HARD LUCK

Another way to plaster your target is by wrapping all or part of his car in the plaster-impregnated bandages used for making emergency casts for broken limbs. Once you've done the first aid, throw a few buckets of water over your handiwork. Choose a fine day or night, and in 10 or so minutes the wet bandages will set like rock.

SLICK TRICKS

No doubt there are some people who would consider the above tactics perilously close to vandalism, so it needs to be said that some of the best tricks require nothing more than for you to create the illusion of there being a big problem.

For example, if you dump a quantity of used engine oil under your target's car, taking care to smear a suitable amount on the sump, your target's bound to think he's got a leak on his hands and will either waste time and money at the garage or disbelieve his dipstick and top up the already full crankcase—and there's nothing quite like overfilling the oil to cause real leaks and splits in the seals. See how easy it is?

Of course, to be really certain your target consistently overfills the oil, simply saw half an inch off the dipstick.

ONE-WAY TICKET

This one relies on your being in the right place at the right time—when your target gets a parking ticket. Swipe the ticket, doctor it in some suitably offensive way—words, pictures, etc., then send it off—without the fine, naturally—to the authorities.

DICING WITH DEATH

Does your target have a pair of those stupid furry dice dangling from his rear-view mirror? Why not replace them with something rather more appropriate to his deadhead mentality: a pair of dead rats or frogs, or perhaps a pair of bull's eyeballs (ask the butcher) or testes.

LIGHT UP YOUR LIFE

Tailgaters can be a real pain in the arse, but there are ways of keeping them off your rear. The simplest method involves rigging up a switch connected to your brake lights. As soon as someone creeps too close to your bumper, flip the switch, and *voila*—it looks like you're braking. More sophisticated avengers might like to hook up a double switch, with the second connected to the reverse lights. Imagine how you'd feel if the car in front suddenly looked like it had been thrown into reverse. Of course, if you're truly nasty, you could rig up one of those ultrapowerful spotlights to the roof rack or bumper. This is especially useful for zapping night-time tailgaters.

MOVING EXPERIENCE

We've all seen movies where the strongman lifts cars—and it's not impossible. Today's small cars can literally be lifted right off the ground, but you'll need more than Arnold Schwarzenegger's two fingers; five fit friends should do the trick. Check the car isn't alarmed, or disable the alarm if possible. Now shift the car to a spot where it's going to be well-nigh impossible to drive it out. Better still, a place where it's also going to be difficult to get into it—between two closely planted trees is ideal, especially if it's only a two-door. Rope in a few more friends and you might even be able to turn it upside-down. Alternatively, move it into a restricted parking area then make a concerned call to your local police station's traffic division. A parking fine is the least your target will get away with.

TOW JOB

On the other hand, why should you do all the work when someone else can do it for you professionally? Look for towing companies in the Yellow Pages and be ready with a suitable story as to why the car needs to be towed away. Make sure you can rattle off salient details about the car, too—registration number, make, and colour—as well as your target's name and address, and, of course, the place you want it towed to, a garage being the obvious choice.

Phone the mechanic in advance, naturally, and for good measure, tell him you don't need the car back in a hurry—that way the scam won't be discovered for a few days. Give the mechanic your target's name and number if you're feeling kind, a false one if you're not. And if you're really vindictive, try to palm the towing bill off on your target, too, by asking the company to send it to his home address.

DRIVE THEM NUTS

Lots of wheels are now fitted with locking wheel nuts as an antitheft device. If your target hasn't yet invested in these, do him or her a favour and fit some for him. Then, either wait for nature to take its course, or help things along by letting down the tyres. Better still, puncture the tyres and put your target in an even stickier situation by gluing up the locking nuts.

If your target has already got locking wheel nuts and you're truly determined, you could replace them with new ones. You'll need a cordless drill to bore the centres out.

The other option, of course, is to simply loosen the wheel nuts, or take them off altogether. The car will go only a few yards before the wheels fall off and your target comes to a grinding halt. Acutely embarrassing.

MAKE A RACKET

Can't be bothered to go to all that trouble? Another way to drive your target nuts is to slip a handful of nuts, bolts, and screws into the wheel well behind the hubcap. The clanking and scraping will convince him the wheel's about to drop off.

CHAIN REACTION

Back on the subject of security, why not give your target the benefit of your concern for his safety? Chain his or her car to a parking meter or lamppost or, for maximum irritation, the car in front or behind. A good sturdy padlock completes the picture and will trigger a whole chain of satisfyingly embarrassing events—and convince your target that somebody out there really cares about him.

Far more devastating is the following piece of rearguard action: buy a good length—12 to 13 yards or so—of quarter-inch Kevlar rope. Lightweight and enormously strong, Kevlar rope has the added benefit of being almost invisible at night. Now, attach one end around both ends of your target's rear axle with a double half-hitch. Leave 8 or 9 yards of slack coiled under the car and tie the loose end to a lamppost, bollard, or other immovable object. The results of this trick are spectacular. By the time the rope pulls tight when your target drives off, the car will have gathered sufficient speed to severely disable or even rip out the rear-end suspension.

Back to chains, another neat trick requires access to the car and works best with two-door models or ones that don't have central locking. Get a good, long length of sturdy chain and pass it from one side over the roof of the car to the other. Now thread the ends through the front seat windows, pull the chain tight inside the car, padlock the ends together, and wind up the windows as far as possible. You'll have to crawl into the back seat to get out and make sure you lock the back doors from inside as you leave the car. Result? Your target will find himself in a real bind, as he won't be able to get into the car without inflicting at least some damage on his precious vehicle.

A more subtle way to tie your target in knots is to use strong sport-fishing line—the kind that can hold a fighting marlin—for a variation on the first tactic. This works best on cars that are parked nose-to-nose. Simply tie the cars together by looping the line several times through the front grills. Whoever moves first will rip out either his own grill or the other car's—and possibly both. Whatever the outcome, you'll have the satisfaction of knowing that your target will certainly come in for a grilling.

TAKE NOTE

Lazy avengers can score a satisfying double goal with one simple note. Write a brief apology along the lines of "Dear Sir, I'm sorry for the damage I've done to your car and will gladly pay for the cost of repairs". Sign it with the name and address of a secondary target and slip the note under the wiper of your main target's shiny pride and joy. Even though you haven't done anything, your neurotic target is bound to anxiously examine every inch of his body-work and, in the process, will probably find a scratch or two he's never seen before. The rest can be left to your imagination.

MAKE IT STICK

A more subtle but also more public way of humiliating your target is to add discreet bumper or window stickers to his car. Starting with the obvious ones, you could affix a Labour Party sticker if you know your target is a rabid Tory, or an ANC flag if his dearest wish is to join Terre Blanche in South Africa. There's plenty of weird and wonderful organisations around that will be only too happy to sell or send you their car stickers, so take the trouble to find one that's really appropriate, or have your own made up. The beauty of this little scam is that it's often quite a while before the offending sticker is discovered, so your target will never really know how long he's been "supporting" the cause furthest from his heart.

Make sure the slur really sticks by coating over the sticker with a permanent glue. If your target is a prominent public figure and his views are well known, you could always double his embarrassment by tipping off the gossip columns. Or take a photo of the sticker in situ and send it to an appropriate magazine or newspaper.

NICE LITTLE NUMBER

Another subtle move is to remove your target's number plates. It's an offence to drive without them and, let's face it, how often do we check to make sure they're there? Fortunately, a policeman has only to look once to nick your target.

ANIMAL MAGNETISM

Anyone who has ever cleaned a car will know that the most difficult naturally occurring substance to remove from the paintwork is bird droppings. So if your target deserves to be shat on, enlist the help of the local bird population by sprinkling the roof of his car with birdseed or biscuit crumbs, and let nature do the rest.

ADD A LITTLE COLOUR

Why not revamp the car with a total respray? Apply water-based poster paint (hot pink, perhaps?) with a spray pump for a professional finish and wait for the colourful language.

Another tactic is to spray-paint only the windows, or, even more subtle, cover the headlight glass with heavy black paint. With a little luck, your target won't discover she's been black-listed until she tries to turn her lights on miles from anywhere that evening.

FINISH IT OFF

Another way to make your target see red is with plain brake fluid—but not the silicon type. Strafe his car with a few good squirts—two coats should be enough—and watch the finish disappear.

For lasting damage, of course, there's nothing quite like the old key-scraped-along-the-paintwork trick. But make sure no one sees you.

NEWSWORTHY

A good way of making sure you get the last word is to cover your target's car in them—thousands of the things. Simply get a stack of newspapers and a big tin of epoxy and slap sheets of newsprint down all over the car body.

A BITTER PILL

Prime targets where cars are concerned are the dodgy dealerships that make car buying hell. If you reckon you've been sold a lemon, there are a variety of ways you put the squeeze on them.

One of the best methods requires a little creativity and is made a million times more simple if you have access to a computer graphics package. Scan in an advert for the car dealership, or, if you're disgruntled with the car manufacturer, for the make and model of car you drive (or would if the damn thing worked). Now, with a little expertise, you can drop in an image of a lemon in an appropriate spot. Have the new image printed up as postcards and either do a mail drop in the area of your duff dealer or post them off with a suitably acid message to various high-ranking executives in the car company's hierarchy. Guaranteed to make them feel sour.

If it's a car dealership you're aiming to shoot down, you could bring new meaning to the phrase "customer relations" by casually dropping a "used" condom (add a little mayonnaise thinned with water), or perhaps a pair of preworn lacy knickers, inside a test model.

The old potato-up-the-exhaust trick could prove embarrassing for them, too, convincing potential buyers that their cars are definitely nonstarters, while the phial of castor oil up the tailpipe will send out steer-clear smoke signals to all and sundry.

Damaging the paintwork is another good trick. Try filling a small water pistol with paint stripper, brake fluid, or a suitably coloured paint, and direct a short, surreptitious burst at every car you pass. In fact, why not get really dirty and pack two pistols—the second filled with used oil? Spray it through the grill onto that sparkly, newly valeted engine.

IT'S A FAIR COP

Revenge professionals know when it's time to take the law into their own hands, but the truly experienced also know when to use it to their own advantage. We've already looked at all sorts of expensive ways to drive your target up the wall, but as a grand finale, why not send him the bill—in person? Perhaps the finest—and easiest—way to embarrass your target is to simply report his car stolen. Phone the police when you know where your target is going to be driving and tell them someone has just nicked "your" car. Give them the direction your target was headed and a description of him and his car. Obviously, you have to make sure you know the registration number, make, and model of your target's car, plus his personal details—name, address, and telephone number.

The very least your target will get away with is a lot of embarrassing explaining, but put this scam into play when you know he's just had a few drinks and he'll experience firsthand the other meaning of the word "nicked".

Clothes

You know the old saying: clothes maketh the man. Well, clothes can just as easily be his undoing. Remember the revenge notorious House of Commons researcher Pamella Bordes exacted on her former lover, *Sunday Times* editor Andrew Neill? When their relationship fell apart at the seams and she discovered she was not his one and only, she decided to vent her anger by cutting rather more than vents in the trousers and jackets of his racks of expensive suits. Lady Sarah Graham-Moon, whose tactics are mentioned in greater detail in the "Relationships" chapter, began an orgy of revenge on her errant husband by hacking a sleeve from each of his 32 tailor-made suits. A bit of 'armless fun', you might say.

There are more subtle ways to stitch up your target, of course. And why skirt the issue when you can make them really shirty? If you've got a lingering animosity you'd like to iron out, here's a wardrobe of ideas to rifle through. You're sure to find one to suit.

PURPLE PAIN

Raid the science lab, your ancient chemistry set, or ask a pharmacist for some methyl violet. Just a touch in your target's washing powder will permanently stain his clothing and go a long way to ruining his wardrobe. Potassium permanganate crystals will also have a violet result, although the problem might be disguising them in the powder. If you don't think you'll get away with it, perhaps the best thing to do is drop the odd crystal down the water reservoir of your target's steam iron. Imagine his horror when he presses the jet stream button and gets a swoosh of deep purple all over that pristine white shirt. Should be enough to turn him purple, or at least puce, too.

POP GOES THE WEASEL

Buttons have an unfortunate habit of coming adrift from the most strategically revealing places at the most inopportune times, but whereas most of us can either haul something else out of our wardrobe or get away with a strategically placed safety pin, military top brass (or anyone who has to wear an ornate uniform) usually have just the one, so they will have to hunt the escaped button down and sew the little blighter back on—or risk looking less than correct.

You can help the pop, pop, popping along by painting a drop of neat bleach or battery acid on the thread at regular intervals (take care not to leave evidence in the form of spilled drops on the uniform fabric). The bleach or acid will quickly weaken the thread to the point where the buttons simply drop off of their own accord when a little extra strain is placed on the thread—something that tends to happen at those inopportune moments. A good way to expose your target to ridicule.

Of course, you save yourself some trouble by simply snipping off all the buttons and throwing them away.

SIDE-SPLITTINGLY FUNNY

Get hold of one of those handy little thread cutters known as Quick Unpicks and use them to unpick a few stitches at regular intervals in the seams and hems of all your target's clothes. Go for the back seams of skirts and the seats of trousers, and the armholes of shirts and blouses. Don't overdo things, though—you don't want the damage to become apparent immediately; rather, you want his or her apparel to fall apart gradually.

A less obvious but equally satisfying scam is to unpick your target's pocket seams—once again, not completely, but enough so that in a very short time he or she begins to lose things.

TAKE THEM TO THE CLEANERS

So, your target has a favourite evening frock or smart suit that he or she is particularly attached to? Make it your business to find out when next it is to be taken for cleaning. Assuming the target hasn't asked for a same-day service and will leave it there for at least a week, get on the phone or write a letter posing as his or her spouse/partner or parent.

Tell the cleaners the target has died (car accident/heart attack, etc.) and that you found the dry cleaning stub in the deceased's wallet. Tell them you'll pay the bill, but, as the dress/suit was your loved one's favourite item, you can't bear to see it again. Ask them to give the article to charity or to throw it out, and reiterate that you really don't want to see it when you come to settle up.

TRULY ILLUMINATING

If your target fancies him or herself as king or queen of the disco, here's a great way to make sure everyone else thinks he or she is actually the fool. You'll need either an invisible security felt-tip (a pen that looks just like a normal felt-tip but whose ink shows up only under ultraviolet light) or, failing that, a solution of crushed malaria tablets (the quinine variety), which also glows under ultraviolet light.

Now find a way to get hold of the target's favourite disco clobber and spend some time writing an appropriately illuminating message or, if you're a little more artistic, drawing something creative onto the back of the garment. Your target, naturally, won't be able to see the result under normal lighting, but next time she gets on down, chances are she'll be laughed off the dance floor as the ultraviolet lights disco designers are so fond of come into play on her newly customised clothing. Now that should bring a glow to her cheeks.

ACID COMMENTS

Nitric acid is a good way to burn holes in your target's wardrobe—and a hole in his pocket, as he'll be forced to replace the damaged articles. Experiment on rags with the acid in various solutions so you'll get an idea of what concentration you'll need for the effect you have in mind. And please bear in mind that the acid burns skin as well as fabric—so make sure your target isn't wearing the clothes when you set to work with your squirter.

STICK THE BOOT IN

Ski wax is used by snow skiers to make the undersides of their skis supersmooth and frictionless for that downhill run. Slicked onto the soles of normal shoes or boots, especially smooth leather ones, it has a similar effect, especially if you pull this stunt in winter and your target happens to tread on a patch of ice. The problem for your target, of course, is that he is probably expecting to have a slightly better grip on the situation. A case of slip-sliding away . . .

BADGER THEM

Button badges might not be as popular as they used to be in the early eighties, when people covered every possible surface of their clothing with the things, but they're still a great way to get your message across. And if your design is witty and colourful enough, you'll find plenty of people who'll be willing to wear them, unaware that they're part of a campaign to discredit your target.

Make up your design—if you have a computer with a good graphics package and access to a colour photocopier, the possibilities are endless—and either have a batch made up professionally (look in the Yellow Pages—T-shirt screenprinters often do a sideline in badges) or make up your own using the kits available in good craft shops.

Now, either post the badges off to your target and her associates, or spread the damage further by handing them out to strangers free. Of course, if the badges are good enough, you might even be able to sell them. Well, there's more than one way to profit from revenge.

SOLE-DESTROYING

If you've discovered that stunningly expensive pair of shoes you took a shine to were actually a load of old cobblers, and the shoe shop you bought them from won't accept responsibility for the shoddy workmanship, let other customers know their business stinks by concocting the following hit.

Liquidise a mix of cheese spread and alcohol in the blender, suck it up into a syringe, and take it along with you next time you visit the shop. Go at a busy time and ask to try on a few pairs of shoes. When an opportunity presents itself, surreptitiously inject a good squirt of the cheesy mix into the inner soles of as many pairs as possible. Put them back in the box as a helpful gesture and exit swiftly. If the shop has an outside display, your task will be made even easier as you can quickly doctor a row of shoes as you pretend to examine them.

No cheese mix? Well a dead mouse is always a good substitute, although make sure you chose styles that will conceal the corpse completely. Whatever you use, the next person to try the shoes on will find they've really put their foot in it—and if the shoes lie around in the stock-room for awhile, they'll practically walk off on their own when the box is finally opened.

If you prefer, you could substitute battery acid for the cheese mix in your syringe and squirt a few drops on the shoes' stitching. This will rot the thread alarmingly quickly, causing more problems for the shop as irate customers return pair after pair of faulty shoes.

ADD SOME ALLURE

Try getting hold of some of the synthetic animal scents used as lures by trappers, hunters, or dog handlers. Some of them smell truly appalling and will leave a lingering odour if sprayed in a fine mist over your target's finery. The right ones, of course, could cause more than a stink. The scent of a female dog in heat, for example, will bring the local male dog population in droves to follow your target in a Pied Piper parody all over town. Perfect if your target's a real bitch.

STICK TO YOUR GUNS

So your target has driven you up the wall. Instead

of cutting up his clothes, why not gum them up? Stick his clothes to the walls, the floor, wherever and however it takes your fancy. Arrange the arms and legs to spell an appropriate message

WHAT A LOAD OF RUBBISH

The following scenario actually happened purely by accident—but the results were so wonderful that it's worthy of being included as a final act of revenge.

The star of the proceedings had recently given his lady love her marching orders. She stormed out, then rang a few days later to say that while she would never set foot through his door again, she wanted her clothes back. She demanded that he pack up her wardrobe and take it into work with him, from where she would collect it.

Our hero, being a gentleman, duly did as was requested, carefully folding her extensive and expensive wardrobe into several large black bin liners, which, the following morning he humped into work. The ex hadn't shown up by the time he finished working that evening, so he stacked the bags by his desk and went home.

Next morning he arrived at his desk to find his corner of the office neat and tidy—and empty. The precious bin liners had been spirited away by the zealous cleaning staff, who most likely assumed the bags of "rubbish" were the result of him being the latest victim of the management's staff-slashing programming.

Distraught, our hero desperately tried to track the bags down, only to be told by the cleaning department that the previous day's rubbish had already been taken away and incinerated.

Even more distraught, he phoned his ex, who, oddly enough, didn't believe a word of his story. Being a gentleman, he coughed up the cash for a new wardrobe—but then he hadn't planned the events as calculated revenge . . .

Entertainment

*T*he most satisfying revenge is that exacted with an element of surprise—that is, when your target is least expecting it. So, when plotting how to get your own back, it makes sense to concentrate on your target's favourite pursuits. After all, who but a total neurotic expects the sky to fall in when he's having a great time? The added bonus, of course, is that in the process of turning your target's fun into funk, you'll have a high old time yourself. So if your target's a keen concertgoer, orchestrate a situation that will make him feel the pits; if he loves the movies, find a way to cause a scene and turn the spotlight of suspicion on him; and if sport's his thing, make sure you even that score once and for all.

WIPE THE SMILE OFF HIS FACE

If your target is a music buff, find a way to access his tape collection and either wipe the tapes with the help of a large horseshoe magnet or tape over them. You can opt for either a suitable message or tracks by their least favourite musician—Mozart or Kylie Minogue for heavy metal freaks, say, or Motorhead (or Kylie Minogue) for those with rather more refined tastes in music. If the tape is a homemade compilation, you'll have no problem over-recording, but if it's a shop-bought cassette, simply place a piece of sticky tape over the two record-protect holes and start work. Do it selectively—a burst here and a burst there and you're bound to strike the right note of revenge.

TALL STORIES

Are you sick of tall people or women with ridiculously "big hair" or, worse, hats, spoiling your view at the cinema or theatre? Take along a small bottle of mineral water and surreptitiously pour it over the seat in front of you. If you're feeling nice, warn people before they sit down that the seat is wet. If not, don't. The results will be the same. Nobody wants to spend a couple of hours with a wet bottom.

If your beef is with the theatre or cinema management, substitute a tin of condensed Hearty Beef and Vegetable or minestrone soup. Those little carrot chunks make it look sickeningly like vomit. Glue and golden syrup will also land the management in a sticky situation.

CALLING CARD

Most people are familiar with that particularly

awful species of greeting card, the musical message card. In place of the usual asinine verse, when you open the card you get a tinny, computerised rendition of "Happy Birthday" or some frightful Christmas carol. Some of you may have even experienced the horror of not being able to get the damn things to shut up. Like cockroaches, the tiny mechanism responsible is almost impossible to kill, so imagine the effect if you were to be assaulted by several of these high-pitched little monsters at once. Get the picture?

Buy several cards and remove the devices from them. Now secrete them in your target's car, home, or office. They're so tiny they'll prove difficult to find, especially if you use your ingenuity in concealing them. Get out of earshot and relax—your target's bound to get the message.

SERVE THEM RIGHT

For matchless entertainment, balls up your target's tennis game by filling a large syringe with plaster or car-body filler and injecting it into her tennis balls. Don't fill them right up—your target will notice the weight. Enough to form a lump the size of a large marble is all you need to unbalance the ball and have her laughed off court. If you can't manage to get hold of her balls, doctor a new pack of the brand she normally uses and substitute it at an opportune moment.

ON COURSE

On the subject of balls, if your target is a keen

golfer, search the joke shops for trick balls. Knutz in London (1 Russell Street, London WC2B 5JD) sells balls that refuse to roll straight, as well as ones that explode or disintegrate in a cloud of dust when they're hit, for a modest £1.99 each. They look fairly convincing, but it's probably best to substitute them part-way through the game when your target would not normally examine the ball too closely.

Another way of sinking his ego as he sinks that tricky putt is to fill up one of the holes on the course with some particularly nasty substance—oil, dog poop, maggots, etc. Make sure you play to lose that hole, though.

WATCH THE SPARKS FLY

Tired of your target's filthy smoking habits or of the overflowing ashtrays in your local pub? Here's a way to illuminate the problem. Buy a pack of sparklers and scrape the explosive coating off the wire stems or snip them into short lengths with wire cutters. Deposit a vial of this material in the loaded ashtrays. Next time someone leaves a burning cigarette or stubs out a butt, he'll set off the fireworks. A sprinkling of magnesium powder, which flares up alarmingly when lit, will provide a further flash of inspiration.

HUBBLE-BUBBLE, TOIL, AND TROUBLE

If your target's entertainment is dope, why not give him a truly spectacular case of flashback? Substitute methylated spirits for the water in his bong and stand back next time he lights up.

Less dramatic, but just as big a blow, is to substitute dried strawberry leaves for his stash of weed—by all accounts they smell just the same when lit. Or you could doctor his resin. Add some sulphur powder (which smells like rotten eggs when burnt) or powdered iodine (which produces lots of smoke) and watch him make a real hash of things.

SMOKE-SCREEN

They say where there's smoke there's fire, but it's more often a cigarette or cigar adding to the pollution. So if your target's favourite pastime is your poison, give her a taste of her own medicine. Using a long, fine needle, thread a few horse or human hairs through one of her cigarettes or cigars. Trim the ends of the hairs and replace the cigarettes/cigars in their packet. The taste and smell is, by all accounts, truly sickening.

SKATING ON THIN ICE

Skateboarders can be pretty selfish in their search for fun. If you've got a troublesome gang of them mowing down pedestrians on the pavements, try scattering a handful or so of large-calibre rifle ammunition primers (available from gun and some sports shops) in their path. When the skateboard wheels hit them, they'll explode with a rather satisfying bang.

SPOIL THEIR VIEW

Satellite dishes are not just an eyesore, they're also a prime revenge mechanism. If your target is a satellite

TV junkie, imagine how distressed he'll be if his viewing schedule is suddenly interrupted. How to do it? Well, there are a variety of ways, some easier than others. As you probably know, satellite dishes need to be perfectly aligned to receive a solid signal, so just a slight adjustment to their position can throw them right out. Move the dish vertically to be absolutely sure you send the target the right signal.

Alternatively, lob a handful of cement or filler into the central waveguide aperture to severely disrupt your target's viewing pleasure. Or paint the entire dish with stone-textured paint. The mesh variety can be messed up with a pair of wire cutters. And if it's Christmas, well, why not dress the dish up with some interfering metal tinsel—what better way to dish it out?

Food

C an't stomach any more of your target? Maybe it's time you turned the tables by turning your thoughts to food. They say if you can't stand the heat you should get out of the kitchen, but sometimes it pays to hang on in there. After all, it's the perfect place to cook up that special recipe for revenge. And if you haven't a clue what to serve, here are a few ideas for starters.

THE EYES HAVE IT

If your target refuses to see eye-to-eye with you, why not send him a memento of your differences—a real eye. Go for fish and sea-creature eyes, such as those from squid and octopus. They're plentiful, inexpensive, and particularly appalling, especially when excised from their rightful owners. Use your imagination in how you deploy them—into gloves, pockets, cocktails, and cups of tea or coffee. Here's lookin' at you, kid.

YOUR CUP RUNNETH OVER

This old classroom trick can be used in homes, offices, restaurants, and cafes: select a cup or mug and find a piece of thin, stiff card or plastic. Fill the cup or mug right up with water, urine, or some other unpleasant liquid, and place the card over the top.

Now press the card firmly against the rim and invert the cup. If it's full enough, the card stiff enough, and the inversion quick enough, you will be able to remove your hand and the card will stay attached to the cup.

Now place the card on the table, apply a downward pressure and quickly withdraw the card. The next person to lift the cup will end up with a flood of your chosen liquid all over them.

GROCER OBSCENITY

Ever noticed how certain fruit and vegetables resemble certain parts of the, er, human anatomy? Well, one wag in Belper did, as *The Belper Express* reported:

"We were disgusted", Ted Varney, a Belper pensioner, told reporters. "My wife's no prude, but finding two coconuts and a massive cucumber arranged in an obscene manner on our car bonnet brought on her shingles. This is the last straw. Last week there was a root vegetable rammed up the exhaust pipe, also in a suggestive manner. We had to call the AA out."

The incident was the last in a series of obscene fruit displays that have been mysteriously appearing on local cars, the work of a prowler known to the police only as "General Gherkin".

"Usually it's just an apple, an orange, and a banana", explained a spokesman, "but now the General's started getting nasty. That last cucumber was over a foot long."

A spokesman admitted that police were baffled but promised that all greengrocers in the Belper area would be interviewed. Obviously someone with a chip on his shoulder.

CHILL FACTOR

Ice cubes can be used to harbour all sorts of nasties, with the benefit that, as it takes a while for them to melt, you have a time-delay effect. Pissed off with someone? Then why not relieve yourself, literally, by adding a couple of urine-based ice cubes to her next Scotch on the rocks.

Alternatively, add a maggot to each little ice cube mould after you've added the water, freeze, then wait for an opportune moment to slip your target a doctored cube—or take a whole bag along to your target's party. Watch the guests squirm when the ice in their drinks starts to melt. Tip: this trick is next to useless if your target is a tequila connoisseur.

WHAT A CORKER

If your target's a wine buff and you have access to her cellar, try the following variation of the revenge extracted by Lady Graham-Moon in the "Relationships" chapter (she delivered her philandering husband's cellar of fine vintage wines bottle by bottle to her rival's neighbours). Soak the labels off the bottles, peel off the distinguishing lead foil from the corks, and mix the bottles up so that no two identical bottles remain in the same rack. Now, that's sure to make your target whine.

MILK OF HUMAN KINDNESS

We all know that milk is good for you—all that calcium and protein—but it's not so good when it's left hanging around unrefrigerated. Try pouring a pint of milk under your target's sofa cushions, into the body of the couch. A couple of days should be all that's necessary for things to turn sour.

Condensed milk is another good ingredient for revenge, especially in winter. Try giving your target's windows a good coating on a particularly icy night. The milk will freeze solid and become virtually impossible to remove until the weather warms up. Condensed milk left hanging around also ends up smelling unbearably bad, so find a way of leaving a tin or two around your target's home, or of spreading the contents on something particularly difficult to clean thoroughly—like the carpet.

CAN OF WORMS

Sometimes the labels on tins of food come off with only the tiniest bit of encouragement. Of course, you can stick them back on again, but imagine what a pain it would be to discover that you had actually reglued a baked beans label to a tin of Whiskers. Get the picture? Ease the labels off the tins in your target's pantry (use a sharp Stanley knife for a clean cut if you have to, or try soaking them off) and reglue them on other tins, mixing them up in the most imaginative way you can manage. Easier still is to just remove all the labels. One tin looks pretty much like another, so your target won't know whether she's opening red salmon or Fido's favourite meaty chunks.

While you're there, why not play swapsies with a few other items? Try substituting sugar for salt and vice versa, hard-boiled or rotten eggs for fresh ones, plaster of Paris for flour, engine oil for olive oil, etc. Oh, and if you substitute baking soda for Coffeemate, you might not eliminate them, but you'll certainly have them eliminating.

Another way of tinkering in the pantry is to forget the labels and simply pierce the lid of each tin with a fine drill. This is especially effective if your target is going to be away for a few days, as the smell of decay that greets him on his return will be really ripe.

SPUD-U-LIKE

If your target is one of life's rotten apples, why not treat him to something even worse? Stored improperly and left to rot, few things smell quite so bad as a bad potato and, if you use your imagination, they can be left almost anywhere—little time bombs just waiting to go off, so to speak.

So, if you've done business with a company whose working practices stink, show the management what you think by dumping a rotten potato in one of their ventilation ducts or wedging one behind the pipes in the bathroom. If it's a work colleague, try dumping one in her filing cabinet, that bottom drawer she scarcely ever uses, or under the seat of her car, if you can manage it.

THE YOKE'S ON HIM

If your target is a member of the microwave-owning classes and you have access to his kitchen, take a dozen or so raw eggs from the fridge (or take along your own, just to be sure of a supply). Place them inside the microwave, set it at high for two minutes, and leave very quickly. It might not be a case of egg on your target's face, but there will certainly be egg all over her microwave—and you know how hard cooked egg is to remove.

Another way to foil them is with aluminium foil. We all know how you are not supposed to put metal containers or foil-wrapped items in a microwave, so why not a place a square of tinfoil under the revolving drip tray inside your target's oven? Next time he turns the dream machine on for a quick snack, the microwaves will do the rest. Result: one zapped microwave, one hungry and unhappy target.

Less harmful but potentially as alarming is to leave a handful of popping corn under the drip tray. Next time your target turns the microwave on, the kernels will do their usual explosive stuff. Corny maybe, but sure to give him a good scare.

THE WORM TURNS

If you're dealing with a real parasite, one especially apt way of dealing with her is to slip her some mild cat-worming pills. Grind them up and add them to a strongly flavoured food to mask their flavour. The result will be nausea and a moving case of the runs.

If you really want to see her squirm, you could superglue the toilet seat and lid to the bowl after you've watched your target eat her doctored dinner.

MUSHROOM MAGIC

People do some embarrassing things under the influence of drugs, and certain mushrooms contain enough mind-altering substances to ensure that whoever eats them stands a fair chance of doing some very embarrassing things. Add them to a salad, turn them into soup, or however you like to use normal mushrooms, and serve the resulting dish to your target.

The effects will take a while to kick in, so hopefully your target will be well away by the time he finds himself away with the fairies. A word of warning: make sure you know your mushrooms—some wild mushrooms are extremely poisonous.

SOUP IT UP

Food and alcohol can be a great combination, but when it's 12 pints of lager and a vindaloo, often it's a case of what goes down must come up. Student accommodation is a prime place for this sort of drastic gastric upheaval and, even if the consumer isn't ill, he's usually so falling-down drunk and obnoxious that he wakes the whole house. If you're sick of your target's antics, why not share your feelings with a few other people—by sharing your target's tendencies to regurgitate everything he swallows?

Buy a couple of tins of extra-chunky cream of vegetable soup, mix them with a can of beer and leave the result to "ripen" in the sun for a day or so. Next time your target goes on a bender, wait till he makes it to his bed then pour your deadly brew all over the toilet and toilet floor. In the morning of course, the whole house will immediately blame your target who, chances are, will have been so pissed the night before he won't remember whether he attempted to drive the porcelain bus or not. It might not stop his disgusting habits altogether, but it might make your house consider rationalising its numbers. As for your target, well, cleaning up his "mess" should sober him up straight away.

SLIPPERY CUSTOMER

If you live in a shared house and are sick of your flatmates helping themselves to your goodies, teach them a lesson. Buy a syringe and use it to inject detergent into whatever it is your thieving flatmate likes to eat. As well as making her foam at the mouth, pretty soon it will work on her insides, making your target powerless to control her bowels.

We also have it on the best authority that a drop of Visine does wonders for constipation, so if you think your scrounging flatmate is more tight-arsed than necessary, why not squirt a drop or two into those snacks she insists on stealing from your food supply?

JUST TEASING

If your target drinks tea all day long, try to get hold of some chewing tobacco. Sometimes it's sold in little bags just like teabags. Once you've got your bagged chewing tobacco, add a few to your target's regular teabag supply. One sip of the resulting brew should have him gagging and might even make him promptly sick.

LIP-SMACKIN' GOOD

Finally, for those of you who have had enough of people who drop by like stray dogs at inconvenient times and expect to be fed, there's a recipe for revenge that's tailor-made to get them out of your kitchen for good. The only ingredients you'll need are a stack of dirty plates smeared with meat fat and your own real mutt (stray or otherwise).

Next time the hungry hordes drop by, have your plates ready. Before dishing up, present the greasy plates to your friendly Fido and get him to lick them clean, saying something along the lines of, "I haven't got time to wash up and he's one of the family, really . . . "

If your inconsiderate "guests" don't suddenly lose their appetites or remember an important appointment, you're probably stuck with them for life. Move to another town.

Gadgets
and Devices

*E*lectrical appliances, like cars, offer myriad ways to get back at your target—and they're even easier to put out of action, with the added bonus that often they're also quite expensive to repair. And that means it makes sense to focus your energy on your target's gadgets. If he's one of those people who simply has to have the absolute latest in electronic wizardry, all you need do is find a way to zap his new toy. But while discovering that his Game Boy isn't game for anything will probably cause him a degree of anguish, finding that the iron is on the blink the morning of that important job interview will leave him crushed in more ways than one.

As we all know, the simplest pleasures are often the best, and taking out that single essential item your target firmly believes he cannot live without— whether it's his Corby Tie Press or the amazing 6-billion-megabyte computer system that runs his burgeoning business—is without doubt the best way to make his life unbearable . . . and the finest way to make your day.

ONE FOR THE RECORDER

Video recorders are wonderful things—but if you've got kids, you'll know the VCR's tape slot is also a wonderful place to hold all manner of things other than tapes, and that some of those things are pretty difficult to extract once they've been shoved in: eggs, for example, are notoriously difficult to get out of anything once they've left the shell, so why not slip a couple of quail's eggs into your target's VCR and see what hatches next time a tape is slapped in?

Dog or cat mess could also mess things up a treat—and bring new meaning to the term "dirty movie". A magnet, even a small one, slipped into the tape slot, will cause all sorts of distortion to the next tape he inserts. Naturally, your target will think he's rented a damaged tape and take it back to the store, who may accept that it got damaged in-store somehow. But when the same thing happens to the next tape, you can be sure that your target will get a pretty poor reception from the video rental shop.

Alternatively, attach a small length of sticky tape to the recording head of your target's VCR (refer to the manual for specific instructions on how to access the head). The modification takes only seconds but can spoil hours of viewing pleasure because, while the machine appears to be functioning normally, the sticky tape prevents electrical contact between the head and the tape, so the TV screen remains blank.

PRIME-TIME REVENGE

If you can get hold of a really strong industrial magnet and have access to your target's television for about five minutes, you can really wreck her view. Turn the set on and place the magnet against the screen. The magnet interferes with the flow of electron particles in the picture tube and will eventually cause a black spot of roughly the same size to appear on the screen so the picture is permanently distorted.

This scam is an especially useful way of getting back at the home-appliance store that sold you a lemon dressed up as technology and then refused to repair or replace it. Go along to their showroom with the magnet in a briefcase or bag and hold it in front of the set on the pretext of examining the picture controls. Do this to as many sets as you can, and maybe the results will bring your target round to your point of view.

ON THE RIGHT TRACK

Another fine way to bring your target into line is to reset his VCR's tracking by twiddling the little tracking knob till the picture is unviewable. Now either glue the knob stuck or saw it off and restick it with a tiny amount of weak glue so it comes off in your target's fingers when he tries to correct the problem.

SPEAK UP FOR YOURSELF

Speakers are astonishingly easy to damage. In

addition to the knitting needle trick mentioned in the "Entertainment" chapter, you could try placing iron filings (cut up steel wool works fine) in the magnet gap. In some cases this will involve piercing the flexible barrier covering the gap. When your target turns his hi-fi on next, he'll have a truly mind-blowing musical experience. Iron filings are also a good way to blow televisions and amplifiers—simply pour some filings into a flexible plastic straw, stick the straw through the ventilation spaces of the appliance, and blow.

FLEX YOUR MUSCLES

The cords on electrical appliances are an excellent target for revenge because they are seldom suspected of being the cause of a problem—the plug, yes, the gadget itself, even, but the cord? What could go wrong with it? Try this: unplug the appliance and shove a dressmaking pin through the flex (through the wires rather than just the covering). Using a pair of wire cutters, clip the protruding ends of the pin as close to the cord as possible so they can't be seen, and plug the appliance back in. Next time your target turns it on, the pin will create a short circuit between the wires. The result will be an impressive flash and puff of smoke and a blown fuse.

Your unsuspecting target will naturally assume there's been a current surge and will dutifully replace the plug fuse, turn the appliance back on, and have the same thing happen all over again. The result will very likely be an expensive trip to the repair shop to try to pin the problem down, so to speak.

PLUG 'EM

Another invisible way to make your target's favourite appliance play dead is to paint the pins of the plug with several coats of clear nail varnish. The varnish will act as an insulator to prevent the current getting through—although perhaps your message might.

SIMPLY STUNNING

Stun guns are handy devices for urban guerrillas who don't like blood; but whereas your average terrorist uses them on people, masters of cold, hard revenge use theirs to stun their targets in a rather less obvious away—by zapping their electrical gear, computers in particular.

How you get hold of a stun gun is your business (try the small ads in *Soldier of Fortune* magazine), as is how you smuggle it in to the target location, but suffice to say these gadgets pack a powerful punch— around 40,000 volts of punch, in fact. Hit a computer terminal with that kind of kick and the effect is, well, terminal, leaving your target with a bad case of microprocessor meltdown and, hopefully, without the vital information he had stored on his silicon-chip chum's hard disk.

Another way of wiping out the hard disk is by reformatting it. Each computer is different, but if you can get access to your target's computer manual, the commands should be in there. If not, make it your business to find out what they are. Most computer manufacturers have friendly user help lines to sort out people's glitches and give advice. And isn't it worth a phone call to wipe out that hard disk—along with the smile on your target's face?

STICKY WICKET

Can't lay your hands on a stun gun? Never mind, you're bound to be able to get hold of some artist's spray adhesive. Now all you need is a second or two alone with your target's 3.5-inch computer disks. These disks incorporate a slide-across protective metal cover, but it's the work of moments to simply slide the metal back (push the tiny tag in the side edge down) to reveal the delicate storage disk. Now spray the tiniest amount of adhesive onto the exposed disk, then let the metal cover close over it again. When the disk is next inserted, the adhesive, which remains sticky, will be transferred to the read/write head of your target's computer, with dire consequences. And if your target tries to check the disk by trying it in someone else's machine, you can bet he'll find himself in an even stickier situation.

Even easier is simply slipping a small magnet into your target's box of disks. Corrupt? You bet.

GETTING DOWN TO THE NITTY-GRITTY

Still on the subject of disks, another way to modify your target's computer terminally is to split open a disk and remove the shiny black storage material inside. Replace it with a circle of fine-grit black sandpaper, and sandwich the disk cover back together again with a drop or two of superglue. Slip the disk among your target's, and wait till the next time he inserts it. When he does, he'll discover exactly what the term "rough justice" means.

THE CHIPS ARE DOWN

A less abrasive way of causing consternation is to simply remove one of the key leads from your target's computer. This can be tricky to spot, especially if her computer is one of several at the workstation, or if the machine is also hooked into printers, disk drives, modems, and fax machines. Alternatively, cause a spot of mayhem by mixing up the leads among several computers. You'll have the satisfaction of knowing that, until the tangle is sorted out, no work will get done.

A more difficult problem to set to rights involves rearranging the computer's chips—the elongated black objects stuck on the circuit board. With the back off the machine, you should be able to access the chips easily. Now simply remove one or more and dispose of the evidence or rearrange them—or coat them with clear nail polish to insulate the connection. That should leave your target feeling far from chipper.

VIRAL INFECTION

If you're handy with computers, you'll know all about the unofficial electronic "noticeboards" that exist, mostly to share useful information but also to give evil-doers the chance to get their hands on killer computer viruses. Once you're connected up to the notice board, you'll see a list of names—most of them fairly innocuous, but the ones you want rather more obvious. You'll find viruses that will destroy your target system on a certain date, ones that will taunt your target with three chances to abort the virus, and ones that will simply wipe or scramble everything.

Once you've got your virus, it's a fairly simple matter to get your target to load it into your target's system. If he is a regular computer user, send it as sample software (that's how the infamous Mozart virus wound up destroying information around the world). Of course, there's always the chance that your target will have a scanner programme loaded into his machine and that your virus will be intercepted, but still—you did try. And he's bound to appreciate your special brand of infectious humour.

Alternatively, why not customise his on-screen messages, so that the "Are you sure you want to delete this file?" query has the addendum "you cheating bastard" tagged on? Be creative—remember, you're trying to freak your target out.

Another option for the target who uses his computer for sales meetings, demonstrations, etc., is to load in one of the fun programmes you can buy either on the computer black market or, more legitimately, through the small ads in computing magazines just before your target is due to give his presentation. Once you've loaded it, make sure that whatever key your target presses will cause the programme to run, and make sure you choose a suitably embarrassing one—some of the computer- generated porn programmes available bring new meaning to the term "graphic".

MAKE HIM WALK THE PLANK

Piracy is the scourge of computer programme manufacturers. So whether your target is making a fortune or simply helping himself to the products of other people's labour by pirating programmes, why not sink his ship with an innocent-sounding but well-aimed letter to the marketing department of one of the larger computer programme companies:

Dear Sir,

I recently purchased a data base programme very similar to your SuperDuper Filemaster. Unfortunately, it did not come with a user manual, but, as the commands, menus, and file formats are identical to your programme, I feel sure your manual would help me get the hang of it.

Accordingly, I would like to buy a copy of your manual. Please send it to me with an invoice for the appropriate amount as soon as possible.

For your information, you might also like to get in touch with Mr/Ms Target (provide address), the producer of the programme I bought, about bulk sales of your manual, as I'm sure that, like me, the people who buy his/her programme would like a manual to go with it.

Yours sincerely,

AN Other
(false/secondary target's name and address)

BITE THE DUST

Do the dirty on your target by drilling holes in the part of her vacuum cleaner that holds the dustbag (if it's an upright Hoover with a cloth bag, making holes is even easier). Poke holes in the disposable dustbag, too, so that next time he switches it on he spreads more dust than he sucks up. You can sabotage the hose as well, by making holes in it, although this will simply reduce the sucking power of your sucker's machine.

DIRTY LAUNDRY

Public launderettes can be a real rip-off but, luckily, because they are often unattended, revenge is easy. Start with the washing machines. If they are coin-operated, try supergluing coins in their appropriate beds in the slide-in trays. This will effectively render them useless without your having to do any obvious mechanical damage. Alternatively, run a bead of superglue around the lid or door of the machine.

Make a colourful statement—and cause a lot of problems for the launderette—by taping a small block of solid water-soluble dye to the inside of the drum of one or all of the machines (despite the signs, how often do you check the inside of a machine really carefully?).

Moving on to the dryer, set it to "hot" and toss in a packet of cheese slices, unwrapped and individually separated, naturally. Put in enough coins to give you 10 or so minutes of drying time (or should that be grilling time?) and disappear. Whoever opens the dryer next will find himself facing fondue. A rarebit of revenge.

ALL WASHED UP

Because people often pop out for a coffee or to do a spot of shopping while their washing whizzes round and round, launderettes are also ideal spots for you to exact revenge on your laundry-using target. While he's away, try adding bleach or acid to his fabric conditioner, or doctor his washing powder with a generous addition of powdered dye (blue is probably best because it will match the powder). A classic case of wash-day blues.

Another truly evil addition is powdered fibreglass. The tiny fragments will get into your target's clothes and then, when he wears them, will work into his skin, causing no end of irritation—but then, that's what he's caused you, isn't it? Naturally, you can also pull these stunts in your target's home.

On the drying front, slip a handful of colourful wax crayons in among your target's whites—and stand by to hear him wax slightly less than lyrical when he returns.

COP THAT

Copper paint is an invaluable addition to the master revenge-seeker's tool-box, as it's ideal for disrupting all kinds of electronic circuitry. Try painting a thin line of the stuff down the insulator of your target's spark-plugs to connect metal with metal, for example.

Do it to one plug in four, and chances are you'll get your target all fired up and have his expensive mechanic scratching his head for ages until he makes the connection.

SQUEAL ON THEM

Radios are pretty innocuous gadgets, but some radio stations can be really hard to handle. If your target is the radio station that broadcasts live from your favourite sporting event, then why not use your very own radio to get back at him?

Secure a seat as close as possible to the broadcasting booth and take along your ghetto blaster, having carefully disconnected the speakers first. Tune the radio in carefully to your target station, turn the volume to high and the tone knob to maximum treble. The result is feedback on a massive scale that the target can do absolutely nothing about. What a scream!

RADIO DAYS

If you've been taken for a ride by the sharks at your favorite beach holiday resort, put the frighteners on them with something they'll understand only too well.

Modify a radio-controlled model boat to carry a suitably realistic model of a shark's fin. Glue the receiving antenna along the fin and then launch it wherever you want to create havoc among swimmers. A few appearances by your mock Jaws could very well spell death to that particular resort.

SEE WHAT DEVELOPS

So your target thinks he's a bit of a hotshot with a camera? Well, why not help with a few hotter-than-hot shots of your own? Buy a roll of the film your target normally uses, take it out of the box carefully, so as not to damage the box, and use the film to copy the centrefolds in a couple of top-shelf publications or the sickest hard-core stuff you can lay your hands on (remember, if you're target is straight it might be nice to go for same-sex porn for added effect). Use a piece of nonreflective glass to flatten the magazine and prevent glare, and be careful to go in close so you can't see the magazine's page numbers or edges of the photos. Now, rewind the film carefully, leaving the end tag poking out of its cartridge as though it were unused. Replace in the box, reglue the open end and leave it where your target will sooner or later use it.

The result will be a roll of double exposures, and, assuming he gets a photo shop to develop the negatives, he could well find himself in the embarrassing situation of having to explain himself to the vice squad.

BOMBS AWAY

Try tracking down empty cases for practice bombs through military magazines or your army surplus store (it's amazing what some of them have squirrelled away). Now plant the "bomb" in your target's garden, in a cupboard, or leave it on her doorstep.

Of course, if you want to go one step further, you could always approximate the real thing. Buy a bottle of drain cleaner granules (sodium hydroxide). Notice how it says to keep it away from zinc and aluminium? Well, pour a good quantity of of the granules into a glass bottle, add a splash of water and a strip of aluminium foil, then quickly slip a large balloon over the neck of the bottle (make sure you observe the safety precautions listed on the back of the bottle). The resulting chemical reaction will release a lot of highly flammable hydrogen gas. Once the balloon is full, remove it from the bottle, taking care not to let the gas escape. Now, tie a length of firecracker fuse around the neck. When you're ready to let off your "bomb", simply light the fuse and run like *&%#. Remember the Hindenburg? Well, this hydrogen-filled balloon gives a fair approximation of that disaster on a somewhat smaller scale.

A REAL TEAR-JERKER

Another extremely useful device for dealing with people you'd rather not have to deal with is a canister of Mace or CS gas. You'll find it difficult to lay your hands on in Britain, but you can cook up a fair approximation of it at home. Mix three parts alcohol with one part of iodine and half a part of salt. Pour this potent mixture into a small atomizer for easy use—and beware of shifting winds.

APPLIANCE SCIENCE

A final suggestion for those of you looking for more vengeful inspiration: the best place in Britain is a shop in London called the Counter Spy Shop, 62 South Audley Street, W1 (open Mon.-Fri. 9.30 A.M. to 5 P.M., Sat. 11 A.M. to 2 P.M.). A gem of a place, it carries everything from sunglasses with mirrored insides rather than outsides (so you can see behind you) to bullet-proofed Mercedes equipped with sophisticated radio locaters in case of hijack to machine guns. The shop's clients include actors, crown princes, and gadget freaks and, its stock list makes 007 look positively poorly equipped. For the person with revenge on his mind, it's definitely worth a visit.

Alternatively, a flip through the small ads of *Private Eye* yields up some interesting gadgets — especially in the bugging line.

Neighbours

You may be close to them physically, but your relationship with your neighbours is not always a meeting of minds. Police complaints files are filled with petty-sounding problems that have driven otherwise-normal people over the edge. There is the tale of the unfortunately named Pitts couple, with their eight children, four Rottweilers, and endless noisy fights. Their neighbours were unable to get them moved from their council house because it was a condition of the Pitts' bail that they stayed where they were. Mr and Mrs Pitt, it transpired, were on bail for arson, and it was revealed that their former neighbours had petitioned to have them removed from their former home for general antisocial behaviour.

Hating thy neighbour is a national pastime. Andrew Saunders in Kent got so fed up with his downstairs neighbours that he drilled holes in the floor and poured petrol over them, while David Linley—no relation to the Queen's nephew—was arrested for victimising his neighbour Margaret Brown. Having complained to the RSPCA that her budgies were too noisy, he informed her teenage son that she was a whore, dumped grass cuttings over her fence and took pictures of her at her washing line.

If you have the misfortune to live next door to the neighbours from hell, don't just move—be moved to action. There are a number of ways in which you can redress the balance of power with the next-door Neanderthals, and rubbish is as good a starting point as any.

BIN THERE, DONE THAT

When your target puts out his rubbish ready to be picked up by the dustmen, liberally cover it in bacon fat or any other meat grease. This will have every animal for miles around fighting over that bin bag, and probably ripping it to shreds and spreading the contents across the target's garden in the process.

You can also take to dumping your target's rubbish in unwelcome places—in other people's gardens, in the kerb under their car, on their doorstep, and so on. Make sure there's always an old envelope addressed to your target so the owner of the rubbish can be identified. While you're at it, you might also decide to add a few extra items to that rubbish bag— pornographic magazines, exotic underwear, chains, and empty syringes, for example.

POSITIVE FEEDBACK

One of the most annoying things a neighbour can

do is to insist on playing radios loudly at all times of the day and night. If polite requests fail, the only thing to do is to make the sound as ear-splitting for them as it is for you. Generate a little electrical interference by removing the suppressor caps from the plug leads of your lawn mower or strimmer and let the crackle of interference curb their interference with you.

INDECENT PROPOSAL

A good way to get back at neighbours is to write letters on their behalf—after all, one thing you do know about them is where they live. Drop a line to a public figure explaining that "you don't normally write letters of this kind" but that you've been attracted to him for a long time and you are convinced you both should meet.

A politician of the same sex should attract heavy-duty attention, especially if those letters get more and more demented and culminate in threats. Letters of this kind tend to be kept on police files.

READ ALL ABOUT IT

You might also consider investing in a subscription to a magazine on your target's behalf— *Razzle* or *Knave* always go down well with the uptight, or maybe they'd prefer *Gay News* or *Zipper*. Whatever you choose, get the name right, but the address ever so slightly wrong—so that the goodies arrive at the neighbourhood gossip's house next door.

KNOCK, KNOCK, KNOCKING . . .

Ensure your target always has a steady stream of visitors by sending on the following whenever they knock at your door: all salespeople, Mormons and Jehovah's Witnesses, odd-job men, estate agents (to appraise his home for sale), and charities (to pick up "donations").

IT'S A GAS

Phone the gas board on your target's behalf to report a gas leak at 3 A.M. Repeat semiregularly for a couple of months.

DRIVE HIM MAD

Call every minicab service in the area and send cars to the target's home every half hour all night. Repeat regularly, and not only will your target lose lots of sleep, but he'll never be able to get a cab when he needs one.

INVITING TROUBLE

If your most-hated neighbour goes away for a few days, send some inviting messages out to the local criminal fraternity. Not literally, of course, but burglars tend to look for signs that a property is uninhabited, and if one were to notice a whole lot of newspapers left on the doorstep and a message on the front door telling visitors that the owner has gone away for two weeks, he may just decide it's worth a closer look. If you can actually shut down the power, your burglar will be even more delighted, as this will put the alarm system out of order. From your point of view, even if the local crims don't accept your generous invitation, this does have the advantage of turning off the fridge and freezer, leaving your target with a stinking mess of inedible food to throw out when he returns.

Finally, if your ministrations take effect and your enemy decides to flee the area, don't drop the issue there. Get his or her new address and print a friendly invitation inviting everyone in the street to a housewarming party for introducing him or herself. Be sure to describe all his/her special interests (Satanism, "swinging", creative stone-cladding) in graphic detail.

GARDENS

Gardens are the perfect place to reap your revenge on a tiresome neighbour. The beauty of them is that, unlike homes, they are usually fairly accessible—at least at the front. So don't be a weed; enlist Mother Nature in your quest for justice and lead your enemy up the garden path . . .

A GRASS ACT

A well-kept lawn is like a huge blank page just waiting to carry that personal message from you to your target, the lawn's owner. The beauty of the well-kept lawn is that it takes an awful lot of effort to keep in perfect condition but can be irrevocably ruined faster than you can say Fisons.

Writing in weed-killer is an effective way to get your message across. Front gardens with a good downhill slope to the road are particularly good for this. Let your imagination run riot and come up with something that really suits the gardener's character. Personal shortcomings are always good or, if your man or woman is involved in local politics, you might even like to leave a message about the prime minister. But if time is short, one big, well-chosen four-letter word will always send him past the point of mow return. Avengers on a budget can mix one part laundry bleach with four parts water to produce cut-price weed-killer.

If you're a bit of a green, you may balk at the idea of destroying plant life just to upset your target. Instead, get plenty of leaf lettuce seeds and throw generous handfuls over the lawn just before a heavy rain. It grows easily and will provide your target with a green salad that'll leave the bitterest of tastes.

Perhaps your gardener has such conservative tastes that his lawn is the focal point of the whole garden and flowers just don't get a look in. Why not add a little local colour by spraying the lawn a shade of your choice? This can be done at night using a backpack spray device, which can be hired from your local equipment-hire shop. A lurid emulsion paint will have the most long-lasting effect. Watching paint dry will never have been so much fun.

Other amusing additions to your target's lawn include pouring liquid laundry detergent over it just before a heavy shower. When the rain comes down it won't just be your target who'll be frothing at the mouth. Cornflakes are another excellent way to start the day. Invest in several boxes and sprinkle generously over that lawn on a rainy-looking evening. When morning comes your target will be feasting his eyes on a lawn full of soggy, smelly cereal that's almost impossible to remove. If the weather doesn't improve, it'll rot the grass. If it turns hot, it'll bake hard. Truly, breakfast cereal has a versatility that Keith Floyd has yet to discover.

Another way of targeting lawn-lovers—especially the kind who like to start mowing at the crack of dawn, regardless of their neighbours' feelings—is to booby-trap the lawn. Buy a pound of 6-inch nails, bend them into U-shapes, and spray them green for camouflage. Then sow them discreetly over the problem lawn, ready for your early-bird neighbour to reap. This trick should nail your inconsiderate neighbour and guarantee you the lie-in you deserve.

Finally, if you can't reach the target's lawn, take aim over the wall or through the gate. A few balloons or condoms filled with a mixture of motor oil and strong commercial defoliant will leave battle scars to break any keen gardener's heart and will ensure that the grass isn't always greener on the other side of the fence.

HOW GREEN WAS MY GARDEN

It's simple but effective. Break into your target's shed or greenhouse and substitute weed-killer for insecticide or plant food. Make sure the weed-killer is a broad-spectrum type and not one of those designed just to kill specific weeds, then sit back and enjoy the poetic justice as your target tenderly murders those prize roses. Pouring weed-killer or defoliant into his hose will also ensure that green is for "go" in your enemy's garden.

SOW EFFECTIVE

Perhaps you'd rather plant than kill. Introducing new plants to your target's garden can be equally rewarding. Planting weed seeds around his newly sown flower beds or vegetable patch is one possibility. So is planting marijuana behind the shed or in a spot he rarely uses and calling the police when it reaches a healthy size. What a dope he'll feel.

SAND BY YOUR MAN

Organise a new feature for your target's garden while he is away. Pay cash for a truckload of sand or gravel and arrange to have it dumped either on his flower beds or all over his lawn.

SAY IT WITH FLOWERS

Local councils usually favour regimented beds of shrubs and flowers in central public sites, in the middle of roundabouts, and so on. The plants are never grown from seed but are planted fully or partly grown, often spelling out some dreary civic message like "Walthamstow: Borough of the Year", "Doncaster: City of Sunshine", etc. It doesn't take much imagination to realise what an impact rearranging these plants could have. You might choose a personal message to your special target, a more general one to the council itself, or maybe even one directed to the prime minister. Don't suffer in silence; spell it out!

PLANT FOOD

Sweeten up your target by feeding his plants for him. Sugar attracts insects, and rancid animal fat attracts rats and mice, so watering your target's plants with sugar water and the ground around them with melted animal fat will have Mother Nature working overtime—not to mention your unfortunate target.

PRIZE LEMON

Is your target one of those characters who takes a pride in growing enormous vegetables that never, alas, make up for his other shortcomings? If the greatest love in your target's life is the massive marrow he has produced for the local garden show, help preserve its bloated beauty by coating it in artist's lacquer. You might run through the rest of his crops while you're there—nice, glossy apples . . . big, shiny pears . . . or even replace items with wax copies. Perhaps he won't even notice until he's bitten into one of them. Another idea is to fleck the crop with paint so that Mr Green Fingers thinks he has an outbreak of disease on his hands. Take inspiration from gardening books to achieve that truly lifelike look.

POOL RESOURCES

If you are fortunate enough to have a target with a

swimming pool, you really don't have to look any further to make a big splash. Pools are expensive things and, as any installer will tell you, they just keep costing, so it's really bad news for your target when he or she has to empty and clean out the pool. With this in mind, here are a few things that add a little colour and life to a swimming pool:

Ordinary cold-water fabric dye such as Dylon is effective—red looks bloody awful, but if you go for blue, there's a good chance your target won't even notice—until he leaves the pool, that is. Then, of course, he'll really feel blue. Go for yellow dye and you can be even more creative. Add a little urine lure—used by hunters—and your target will wonder who the hell's taking the piss.

If you have any recently deceased animals to hand, give them a burial at sea, courtesy of your target's swimming pool. Failing a corpse, any old crap will do—literally. But if you don't fancy handling the real thing, just unwrap and throw in a few chocolate bars. Lion bars and Picnic bars are particularly realistic, especially if accompanied by bits of "used" toilet paper. Sweet revenge, indeed.

Another slick idea is to pour a gallon of motor oil into the pool. Though beautifully simple, your target will have to buy new filters, flush his lines and pump, and completely clean out the pool—not cheap. Let him know he's been deliberately sunk by leaving a toy oil tanker for him to find at the bottom.

If your target has drained his pool and will shortly refill it, you have the opportunity to make him feel a real prick. All you need are some drawing pins, powerful waterproof glue, and some paint that matches the inside of your target's pool. You can imagine the recipe. Coat the pins in glue and leave to dry, then glue them into place in the shallow end of the pool—especially around the steps. Your target won't know he's been spiked until he puts his foot in it.

Finally, if your neighbour is an ostentatious show-off and is irritating you with noisy pool-side parties and inconsiderate behaviour, instead of polluting his pool, why not simply relocate it? All you need is a long hose, a jug, and a funnel. Put one end of the hose in the water and stick the funnel into the other end of the hose, holding it high above the level of the pool. Fill the jug from the pool and pour it into the funnel, you'll notice bubbles coming out of the other end of the hose as the air is expelled. Keep going until those bubbles stop coming out, then head toward your target's house. It's up to you to decide where you think the pool can be moved most appropriately—to that basement games room, his study, or just wherever you can find an open window. The sight of all that water will be enough to dampen even the flashiest target's spirits. Soak the rich!

Phones

When BT launched its "Make Someone Happy" campaign, it probably didn't even consider the sheer exhilaration the telephone can afford someone bent on revenge. It is the most direct route into a person's home and, as such, is among the subtlest and most lethal tools of revenge. On one level, it can disturb your target from his or her bath; on another, it can jeopardise his or her marriage, bringing unpleasant news into the heart of the happy home. It allows you to be creative, too—as the caller is never visible, it is the natural medium of the actor or actress. So move over, Maureen Lipman, and let the phone make someone—yourself—happy today.

OUT OF ORDER

If your target relies on the telephone, hit her where it really hurts. The simplest way of putting someone's phone out of order is to call her number, wait until she picks it up, and then just walk away without hanging up. She will not be able to use her phone until your phone is hung up or until the telephone company—alerted, of course, on somebody else's telephone—has sorted the problem out. For best results, use a public phone in a very quiet, out-of-the-way place.

NAIL THEM

If you want to put a phone out of order more permanently—and completely confuse the repairman at the same time—unplug the phone, paint over the contact with clear nail varnish, and replace it in the socket. Your target will have even more trouble than usual getting through to people.

YOUR NUMBER'S UP

If you have access to your target's push-button phone, there are a number of amusing ways in which you can set his alarm bells ringing. Unplug the phone, open it up, and look for the button-to-board connections. On modern phones these are usually tracks on a circuit board or ribbon cable. Cut one or two of the tracks or wires, and that digit will fail to register whenever it is dialled. If you are feeling really ingenious, you could even solder on a small jumper lead to one of the other number connections so that, for example, every time your target thinks he is dialling 2, he's actually dialling 7, and so on. You might also disconnect the bell so that incoming calls just don't get answered. Hell's bells!

If you know a particularly rude person who uses his mute button in order to make comments about his caller to those around him, you might think justice would be best served by letting the person at the other end in on this private conversation. All you have to do is find the mute button connection and, snip! Suddenly your target is being more honest with people than he ever thought possible.

HOT GOSSIP

If you just want to make your enemy look a prat, apply a layer of instant self-tanning sun cream—the white, clear stuff that changes colour rather than the brown goo you can actually see—to the telephone ear-piece. If your target is known as a brownnose, you may even change her reputation.

BOMB DEALS

Turn your target into a terrorist. Using his or her phone, make a call to a large organisation, informing management of the fact that there is a bomb in the building. Then make a dash for it leaving the phone off the hook. It is unlikely that your call will be taken seriously unless you know the IRA's current set of code words; however, your target will probably have to explain why he's wasting police time—if he's lucky. If not, there will be a court case and a huge fine. Terrorism is costing the government a lot of money—a friend of ours accidentally left a cake on the tube and brought the whole system to a standstill—so hoaxers are not treated with a great deal of patience. Don't get caught.

CHARITY BEGINS AT PHONE

Those TV telethons are marvelous things, raising all that money for good causes. If you know your target's credit card number, why not make a generous donation on his or her behalf come next Red Nose Day, or whatever? Phone from a public phone and hang around a while, as they sometimes call back to confirm larger donations. If you're smart, you'll choose a sum that's more than your target would ever have donated, but small and affordable enough to make it embarrassing to refuse to pay—between £30 and £75, depending on your target.

PHONE HOME

Phone your target's best friend/employer/parents and, in your most thuggish voice—you may need to enlist special help for this—say something like:

"Your friend Target owes Big Phil Watts two grand. He says you'll take care of it today, personally. So Slasher Harris and Mad Dog MacCarthy are gonna be there in two hours to get the money off you, awright?"

A variation on this theme, suitable for a young target, is to get someone younger, but shrill, angry, and with an equally unpleasant-sounding voice to phone the target's parents. When he finds the target is not at home, he should ask to leave a message:

"The message is that I paid for my dope and that

little creep/bitch had better deliver it or we're gonna come round and rip his/her face off. Either I get my dope today or that little AIDS-bait son/daughter of yours is dead."

HELP AT HAND

Need help dealing with a particularly troublesome target? Call a helpline. A call to the Samaritans from your hysterical target to the effect that he's taken poison, is going to blow up the neighbourhood with a TNT bomb in his flat, and will shoot anyone who comes looking for him should have the boys in blue round in no time. They'll have to tear up the flat looking for the bomb and will probably stick your target in a straitjacket prior to getting his stomach pumped. They won't be very gentle, and their mood won't improve when they find out it's all a hoax.

Women's refuges know how to deal with antisocial types; they have them ringing up all the time. If your target is a particularly evil bully, this will probably suit him. Have a male friend ring the local women's refuge. He should sound slightly drunk, surly, and foul-mouthed. Keep asking for the target's wife by name; mention the target's name, too, as it is "him" making the call. Insist the attendant is lying when he or she says that the woman is not there. Tell the attendant to get her on the phone or you'll come down there and bring her home your own way. Get really nasty. Threaten to burn the place down. Threaten to rape everyone there. Make lesbian charges. Laugh when the attendant threatens to call the police and say you have an axe and explosives. Keep mentioning the target and his wife.

Wait 15 minutes before calling back. Your caller should sound all sweetness and light. He can't apologize enough—cry a little. This is the pattern men of this kind follow. Your caller should accept the counselling for a while before working himself up into a rage again, getting more militant about a man's rights and her lies, etc. If you've given them enough clues, the police should be round at the target house before too long. This works best on bullies who have girlfriends but live alone.

TAKE THE WIND OUT OF THEIR SALES

There's nothing more maddening than sitting down to a meal with friends, only to be summoned to the phone to listen to a salesperson who won't take no for an answer extol the virtues of double glazing. If you are anything other than rude, these people are trained to regard this as a positive response and will probably—even if they don't get an order this time—phone back again and again.

One way of ensuring they don't call back is to listen for a while, then ask a series of questions, sounding more and more excited each time. After about about five minutes, give a heavy moan, scream, "Oh yes, yes. I'm coming." Then clear your throat and say, in your normal voice, "Thank you very much. That felt so good, Thank you." This usually upsets callers of the same sex even more than callers of the opposite sex.

The poor drones who do the calling, however,

really aren't the ones to blame. These are tough times, and people earn a living however they can. Your best target is the fat-cat businessman behind it all. Find out the name and address of the company pestering you as well as the name of the boss. See if you can find out where he lives. If you can, the local telephone directory should furnish you with a telephone number. Then telephone your target remorselessly. Offer to make him a lifetime member of the Pet-of-the-Month Club, try and sell him made-to-measure condoms, offer him double glazing, your wife's home-made cakes, anything. Phone in the middle of the night and offer to sell him sleeping pills. Don't bother to disguise your voice—you want him to feel persecuted. When he finally asks you why you're doing this, tell him—and arrange to have your name and number permanently removed from his company's books.

One final suggestion for dealing with telemarketers is to invoice them for your time and use of your equipment. Listen to the sales representative long enough to find out the name and address of the company involved, then send this:

Dear telephone solicitor
and electronic trespasser,

This is to advise you that on _____ at _____ your representative_____ used our leased telephone line and our telephone equipment. We lease a phone line and purchase equipment to serve our needs. We do not wish to be called by businesses at inconvenient times with unwelcome proposi-

tions. Accordingly, you are hereby charged a £___ line and equipment-access fee for use of our telephone. An additional fee will be charged for all additional calls. Please remit promptly to ___. Failure to remit promptly will result in legal action to establish the right of a citizen to charge access fees to businesses which use a client's leased and owned property without permission.

DISTANT VOICES

Abroad? Make your target wish he were, too, by calling him collect from your destination. Say it's his brother John or sister Jane calling (make sure you know the name of someone he'd definitely take a call from). Then, when he accepts the call, just put down that receiver—don't hang up, just leave it hanging—and walk away. Let's face it, it'll be a while before your target can explain to the relevant authorities what has happened, especially if there's a language barrier.

SURPRISE CALLERS

If you just want to wind someone up, enlist the help of a few friends and get them to call your target's number throughout a day when you know he'll be in. They must all ask for the same person, a fictitious character of your own choice, say, John Evans. After several hours, your thoroughly pissed-off target should get one final call: "Hello, is that (target's first name)? This is John Evans here. Any calls for me?"

Alternatively, using the telephone directory, make about 200 calls and ask for the person listed. With luck, in at least 50 cases they won't be in but there will be someone there to take this message: "Please could you get (name of person listed) to phone (name of target) back any time after midnight tonight. Yes, it is very, very important or I wouldn't ask you to call so late."

To check out your success, why not make a call to that number yourself at about 1:30 A.M.—if you can get through, that is.

Another one is to call a selection of people from the telephone directory and, after making them identify themselves, read out a written statement along the lines of "Congratulations, (name of person), you have won the (name of least-favourite radio station or newspaper) free telephone sweepstake. This is not a gimmick or a sale. Our computer has selected just five names at random from the electoral register, and yours is one of them. To collect your £5,000 cash prize, call (target's phone number) and ask for (target's first name)." Your target won't be the only one who'll feel like a loser.

HOT NEWS

If you want to make sure your target's the talk of the town, why not set alarm bells ringing with his or her neighbours? Phone the neighbourhood gossip and identify yourself as a newspaper reporter. Ask the gossip if she can tell you how long Ms Target has been running a brothel in her sitting room, or whether, in her opinion, Mr Target seemed like the kind of man who would flash at small children in the park. You'll be amazed how quickly these ugly rumours get about.

HELL'S BELLS

This is a really nasty one and should be reserved for the truly evil. From a public phone, call (or get a vicious-sounding friend to call) your target threatening violence, mutilation, and even death. Threaten other members of the family or perhaps a pet that your target is particularly fond of. Make it very frightening and very graphic, but whatever reasons you give for the call, don't mention the real reason (you don't want to get caught, do you?). When you've finished, hang up and don't call again for several weeks. After this, your target will probably call the police, and a trace may even be put on the line. Your next call several weeks later will be altogether different in tone. Phone one of your target's relatives, a spouse if he or she is married, and say something like, "Mrs Target? I am Dr Smith. I'm so sorry to have to tell you this, but your husband has been seriously injured in an accident. Could you please make your way to (name of local hospital) and tell them who you are at the desk?" The beauty of this is that your target and his family will be even more terrified when they find out it's a hoax.

GET THE MESSAGE

Ansaphones are antisocial creations. All they mean

is that you the caller pay for the privilege of finding out that the person you wanted to speak to isn't in—something you could do for free if he or she didn't have an ansaphone. The most irritating people of all are the ones who use their ansaphones to screen their calls like some electronic secretary, listen to your voice, and decide whether or not they feel like speaking to you. Get your own back by leaving an irritating and confusing message. Here are a few suggestions:

Say nothing at all, and leave the phone off until you've used up the tape. Your target won't get any calls and, with any luck, may even think the machine's not working and get rid of it.

Phone repeatedly and fill the tape with your most uneasy-listening music, highlights from the Sunday-morning service, a recording of static noise, or the Margaret Thatcher record version of the Gettysburg address. Your target will have to listen to at least part of each of your calls to check that there isn't an important one among them.

If your target is married, get someone of the opposite sex to leave a compromising message along the lines of: "Hi darling, I managed to get your phone number from your office. I don't know why you're being so secretive—we love each other, don't we? Call me today, I've got something really important to tell you. Love you, 'bye!"

Is he a family man? Get a male voice to leave this message. "Ah, Mr Target. Sorry I've missed you, but our mutual friend is keen to see the pictures you mentioned. I've told him what a little beauty (name of target's child) is, and he can't wait to teach her/him some new games. I'm sure you understand.

If the fee we discussed is a problem, I'm sure we can come to a new agreement, but please call me back soon. Thank you."

If you have access to your target's home, you might like to substitute your own prerecorded message tape for your target's. Reasons for being unable to come to the phone might, for example, include something messy and biologically unlikely with the family cat. Or you may prefer to make your message rude but plausible. This is particularly effective if the ansaphone is used for business calls.

You may not even need physical access to your target's ansaphone to hear his or her messages and even change the message. Lots of modern machines respond to touch-tone digits that can be keyed in at any telephone. Once you have your target's model, the details of how to operate it are readily available from any telephone retailer.

WRONG AGAIN

Finally, how do you deal with those wrong numbers that always interrupt at life's most crucial moments? Don't just scream "WRONG NUMBER!" and hang up; make yourself feel better by making the caller feel worse. Next time you get a strange voice asking for Darralyn-Anne, pause a moment, then, with a slight catch in your throat, whisper, "Oh God, you don't know. Darralyn-Anne has just died. I'm a neighbour and we're all in shock. She's gone (sob). Please don't call here." *Then* hang up.

Post

Whatever your target's done to you, one of the most effective means of ensuring that he or she gets the message is the mail. Yes, friendly Postman Pat can become your instrument of evil, delivering that killer blow come rain, hail, or snow—and all for the price of a first- or second-class stamp.

You will need a few special items, however. First up, you'll need access to a typewriter that cannot be traced—a word processor with laser or bubble-jet printer is better because the typeface is uniform, unlike the more idiosyncratic manual typewriters whose characters are like fingerprints and therefore, if things get hot, could possibly be traced back to you. Second, you'll need a stock of your target's letterheads. If you can't get your hands on a bundle of them, find a way to get hold of at least one and have it copied, either by a printer or on a high-quality colour copier. Third, you'll need official-looking window envelopes, and fourth, a selection of rubber stamps and ink pads.

With the basic kit assembled, it's time to get to work proving that the pen is indeed mightier than the sword.

WRITE ON

With your stack of letterheads at the ready, it's an easy matter to "become" your target. Based on what you know of your target, start writing letters that will cause him maximum embarrassment or loss of face.

For example, if your target is a scoutmaster, have him write to the local newspaper in support of gay rights. If it's the vicar you want to see in hell, have him send a letter to an appropriate—and widely read—magazine in favour of satanic or pagan rituals. If it's the local politician that gets up your nose, write a letter in his name to the National Front, praising his stand on racial issues and offering to stand for his party at the next elections.

In your target's guise, write to government officials and other people in the public eye in the most obnoxious, outspoken terms, demanding the most ridiculous things. Or, alternatively, use the name of a secondary target to vilify your main target. Write a "good citizen" letter to the Inland Revenue alleging that your target is dodging tax or fiddling their VAT. Or that he's fraudulently claiming mortgage relief or income support. Then wait for the heavy mob to descend.

CATALOGUE OF DISASTERS

The bane of many shopkeepers' lives is the customer who comes in, asks endless questions about a product, then announces she is going to buy it from a cut-price catalogue. If you're plagued by one of these troublesome time-wasters, why not give her a few more ideas on how to spend her money by sending her catalogues by the truckload?

Here's how to do it. Have a rubber stamp made up with the words "Please send your free catalogue to:" followed by your target's address (there are some companies that specialise in this—look through the Yellow Pages or ask your local stationers. Next, buy a stack of plain postcards, and then every time you see an advert for a catalogue, send off one of your cards. The advantage of this is that not only will your target be inundated with unwanted catalogues, but because her name will probably find its way onto other mailing lists via the companies you approach on her behalf, the effects will be multiplied many times over. Just what the doctor ordered.

ORDER, ORDER

Use catalogues to your advantage, too, by ordering especially suitable or embarrassing items for your target: haemorrhoid cushions if he's a pain in the arse, nose-hair clippers if he gets up your nose, or incontinence pants if she's pissed you off once too often. Better still, "slip up" with the name on the order and have that bulk order of ribbed glow-in-the-dark condoms and a 10-inch double-action Mr Satisfaction dildo sent to your target's spouse.

Unless you've got a bottomless pocket, make your selection from catalogues that send goods on approval and give you 14 days to return them before sending out an invoice (try to time delivery for when you know your target will be on holiday for a fortnight or more). That way she has to pay for a pile of rubbish she has absolutely no use for. A nice way to disorder your target.

HATEFUL MAIL

If you can't be bothered to go to all the trouble of selecting items to send your target, why not just sign him up to receive junk mail from sources he's likely to find really offensive? Get your unfriendly local butcher on the vegetarian society's mailing list, for example, or the leather shop that sold you a dud jacket on the antifur league's list, or the pro-choice person on the pro-life lobby's propaganda list.

THE CHEQUE'S IN THE POST

So, you've managed to fill your target's letter-box with all sorts of rubbish—but what do you do about the snowdrifts of junk mail that keep coming through your own front door every day? It's well-nigh impossible to have your name deleted from a free mailing list once it's on there, but there are a few ways you can try to convince these postal terrorists to stick their circulars somewhere else.

If the mailshot is a request for money, send them some—Monopoly money, that is, or better still, one of those irritating bogus cheques certain companies send out along with the letter that goes, "Congratulations, you have may already have won £1 million. To find out if you have, simply . . . "

Whatever you send—even if it's nothing—make sure you use their postage-paid envelope.

WEIGHTY WORDS

On the subject of postage-paid envelopes, why not use them to show the senders of all that junk mail what you really think about them? Get one of those special Royal Mail cardboard boxes and fill it either with junk mail from other companies and a note pointing out what a drag it is to receive unsolicited post or with dried dog or cat droppings or cow-pats. Stick the post-paid envelope on top and mail the package. Alternatively, if you want to get heavy (and make an impression on their postage bills), fill the box with a couple of pounds of rocks or sand, or bags of sugar or flour.

Another option is to stuff the prepaid envelopes with some pornography (the more offensive the better) and post it back to the company's HQ. Better still, find out who the boss of the company is and mail it to him or her personally.

WHAT A LOAD OF RUBBISH

One final use for junk mail is to get your target into trouble. If you have access to your target's mail, sort through and collect up all the junk mail until you have a big bag of it (given the amount that comes through most people's doors, this shouldn't take too long). Once you have a bin liner full, take it along to a local beauty spot and dump it or drop it in the gutter or down the drain. Now, good citizen that you are, phone the council and report that you saw someone dumping a bag of rubbish in that spot. Once the rubbish is retrieved, of course, it will be a simple matter for the authorities to find out who has left it there—your target's name will be all over the unopened junk mail. A good way to tidy things up, no?

PRIVATE AND CONFIDENTIAL

One thing you can be certain about is that in an office, nothing stays confidential for long. Even if the office gossip can't find out exactly what's going on, there's nothing like a bit of speculation and innuendo to liven up a dull day. And once the rumours start going round, it's very difficult for the subject to clear his or her name entirely.

So, if you want to cause your target some office anguish, why not send him a few private and confidential letters? Use the long brown envelopes used by many government departments and either print the name of a fictitious but embarrassing sender or, for a more professional touch, have a rubber stamp made up with the source, e.g., "Herpes Test Centre", "XYZ Sexually Transmitted Diseases Clinic", "Home Office-Work Release Programme", or even the name of a competitor company—whatever takes your fancy, basically, but make sure it's as intriguing as possible.

Now fill the envelope with a piece or two of blank A4 paper to give it some bulk and send it off, observing the usual rules about never sending it from a place where it could be traced back to you. If possible, time the posting to coincide with your target's being away for a few days, giving time for plenty of people to see the envelope sitting so innocently on your target's desk and for the rumour mill to creak into action.

Alternatively, send a postcard with a terse but pointed anonymous message: "She's no longer at the topless club, but her colleagues say she went to Manchester . . . can pursue it if you wish", "Sending a cheque to pay cost of half the 'operation'", "Time and money running out . . . you'll be sorry". That should get everybody thinking.

JUST MY IMAGINATION

While you're thinking about thinking, one of the best ways to get at people is to give them only half the story—it fires their imagination and, done cleverly enough, can trigger the latent neurosis that lurks in just about everyone. By post, you can play all sorts of mind games.

Try sending blank letterheads from the Inland Revenue or some other official agency that might conceivably cause your target to lose sleep. Even better than blanks, send the "second" page of an official letter—just a line or two of type with a suitably enigmatic but threatening tone, such as: "If you do not comply with our directive, we will be forced to take matters further." Send follow-ups if the first one doesn't make your target sweat. Mail-icious? Well, that's revenge for you.

MAKE THEM EAT THEIR WORDS

Bogus discount coupons or offers are another satisfying way of getting at your target. Send them a letter entitling him to dinner for two at a local restaurant (possibly your secondary target) upon presentation of the enclosed coupon. Add a sentence to say that booking is not necessary.

Alternatively, send him samples through the post—for example, a bottle of engine oil additive, suitably doctored with abrasives. This is a particularly effective way of enacting some of the engine-damaging ploys outlined in the "Cars" chapter and spares you the grind of having to somehow gain access to his motor.

DEAD LETTER OFFICE

If you want to cause major disruption in someone's life, try filing a change-of-address notice. This is surprisingly easy: simply go along to the target's local post office and ask for a change-of-address form. Fill it out with her address, the forwarding address (Timbuktu, perhaps?), and the amount of time she wants her mail redirected (one month to a year).

You don't even need proof of who you are, although as a precaution it might be wise to do your homework beforehand and have an envelope addressed to your target in your possession (easily done—lightly pencil your address on an s.a.e., post it, then, when you receive it, rub out your address and ink in theirs. *Voila*! One authentic franked envelope). Think of the bills that will go unpaid, the interest that will mount up, the business that might be lost, and the wild goose chase your target will be sent on. Now that's what I'd call first-class revenge.

HIT THE SPOT

Get right to the point with a bogus letter that zeros in on your target's weakness. For example, if he has a nasty case of acne—or even just the scars—and you know he's sensitive about it, send him a letter, on an appropriately mocked-up letterhead, along the following lines:

Dear Target,

As the leading publisher of popular medical texts dealing with unusual problems, we are inviting you to share your experience of (name the condition) with our readers. We know how distressing the condition can be and would like to give fellow sufferers among our readers hope that, despite such disfigurement as you have suffered, it is still possible to lead a near-normal life. In addition to interviewing you, we would also like to photograph your condition. Naturally, if you agree to participate in this project, you will be paid for your contribution.

Yours sincerely,

AN Other
Editor, Medical Division XYZ Books

Spot on, or what?

RETURN TO SENDER

Rely on the Royal Mail to do a royal job of helping you exact revenge on your target by buying a sexy bra and stuffing it in one of the carefully purloined company envelopes used by your target. Add a note (disguise your writing, or type it) along the lines of, "Here's a little something you forgot last night—glad I remember everything we did down in the car park". Address the package to a fictitious woman at a fictitious address and wait for the sorting office to return the envelope to its "sender". With any luck, your target will open the package in full view of someone, or his secretary will open it. Guaranteed to make your target pray for delivery.

CUSTOM-MADE REVENGE

With the help of a desktop publishing outfit, coming up with extremely convincing official-looking forms is easy—especially if you print them on a laser printer using coloured paper. Try something along the following lines to make your target nervous:

NOTICE OF SEIZURE

Please quote the Customs reference number shown below in all correspondence:

Customs reference number: 66/43-87/8763

To: date:

(target's name)
(either stamped or written in by hand)

Dear Sir/Madam,

The parcel described below has arrived here addressed to you. It does not comply with the statutory requirements of the Customs and Excise control of the (Pornography/ Drugs/Firearms) Act of 1989. The parcel and its contents are liable to forfeiture under Regulation 12 Paragraph 5. As required by law, I hereby give you notice that the items specified below have been seized accordingly.

You are further required by law to appear at this office at the earliest possible opportunity to discuss the matter and, if applicable, make representations regarding your position in law. It is an offence under the Act not to comply with this notice within seven days of the above date. It is recommended that you bring a legal advisor with you.

Yours sincerely,

AN Other
Chief Customs Officer

DESCRIPTION OF SEIZED GOODS

Reference number 66/43-87/8763

*Parcel number*_____
*Office of origin*_____

*Date sent*_____
*Name of sender*_____

Contents (pornography/drugs/weapons)

*Contents code**_____

* Please quote the goods category in any correspondence or communication with this office.

C1HH3 F8744 TLH/66/43-87/8763

_____

Now if that doesn't give your target a seizure, I don't know what will.

SECOND-CLASS CITIZEN

If your new neighbour is getting on your nerves and shows no signs of improving his behaviour, try the following. Mock up a letter from the Home Office, saying your target is participating in an early release programme for child molesters/sex offenders/arsonists and that, although the individual is unlikely to reoffend, the slightest indication that he or she is lapsing into bad habits should be reported. Alternatively, say your target is part of the Department of Health's Care in the Community programme, and that while he or she is mentally stable at the moment, the continuing support of the neighbours will be vital to the success of the rehabilitation. Make several copies and distribute to your target's near neighbours.

Given the prejudices of most people when it comes to offenders and the mentally ill, either one of these letters should ensure your new neighbour is well and truly shunned, and you can bet this person will become the prime target of the local Neighbourhood Watch scheme.

BOX OF TRICKS

Stealing mail is not only tacky, it's illegal. Instead, why not remove your target's mail box? If she has an outside post-box at the end of her drive, it's a simple matter to spirit it away in the dead of night. Leave an official-looking notice along the lines of "Your post-box has been removed by order of the Postmaster General in compliance with regulation P/B548-91. Please contact your local post office for further instructions." This ploy is especially effective if your target has a particularly "decorative" post-box.

Alternatively, you can opt to decorate the post-box yourself. Seal up the letter-box, paint it, stick things on it, or simply put something inside—dog turds, large toads, mice, rats—dead or alive—or even a mousetrap are some items that come immediately to mind. Use your imagination.

POST-TRAUMA STRESS

The final method of causing your target grief is an oldie but still a goodie—the old dead-animal-in-the-post trick. Find yourself a nice corpse on the roadside, package it up in an airtight container so it won't leak (or smell), and send it to your target second-class to give it extra time to ripen. If you can't bring yourself to pick up something that still resembles a three-dimensional animal, go for one of those utterly flattened corpses that has been run over and desiccated to the degree that it's become as stiff and brittle as a cowpat. The added advantage of these two-dimensional little beasties is that they cost a lot less to mail but are just as horrifying to pull out of the jiffy bag.

Relationships

*L*ove—it can be heaven and it can be hell—but for revenge experts, the important thing to keep in mind is that no matter how bad you're feeling, there are always plenty of ways to make your ex feel even worse. But then, isn't that what true love is all about—giving more than you receive? So if Cupid's dart has left you wounded, here are some ideas to help you even the score with a bull's-eye on your target.

THROW THEM TO THE DOGS

The opening word has to go to the woman who first made men realise they couldn't get away with bad behaviour—Artemis, the Greek goddess of hunting and chastity. When the hunter Actaeon shamelessly ogled her and her nymphs while they were bathing naked, she didn't blush and waste time feeling humiliated. Instead she turned him into a stag and set his own pack of hounds on him. The dogs dutifully hunted him down, tore him to pieces, and ate him alive.

Such omnipotence is rare indeed these days, and setting your pooch on the man who has offended you is likely to land you—and the mutt—in a lot of trouble. On the other hand, you can throw your target to tabloid newshounds with relative impunity.

The more lurid dailies are always looking for salacious tales of relationships gone wrong—look how they lapped up the stories about Prince Charles and Princess Diana's marriage—and if you don't mind a bit of notoriety yourself, you could ensure endless embarrassment for your ex.

HEARTBURN

Chances are, no matter how discreet he thinks he is, if your partner's cheating on you, you'll find out—and when you do, it pays to be prepared. If you can find out the name of his new paramour, and how to contact her, it's an easy matter to set the ball of revenge rolling.

Posing as your partner, send a brief note to the lover asking her to meet for a secret dinner. Hint, if you like, at divorce, starting a new life together, etc. Nominate the time and place and include an explanation as to why the love-birds shouldn't make contact beforehand (for this ruse to succeed, it's vital your cheating spouse stays out of the picture).

Phone the restaurant 15 or so minutes after the appointed hour and ask for your partner to be paged. Naturally, he will not be there, but there's a good chance his lover will take your call. Play the rest of the conversation by ear, remembering that you have the advantage of surprise. She probably won't stick around for dinner but, not to worry, your target will be too busy digesting how on earth you knew where they were going to meet.

SUSPICIOUS MINDS

Give your cheating partner something to think of other than her next tryst by "accidentally" leaving a lipstick-smeared tissue (if you're a man) or an empty condom wrapper in the bathroom bin. Go further by leaving a pair of sexy underpants (if you're a woman) or knickers (if you're a man) under their pillow or at the foot of the bed. Less obvious but equally potent "evidence" includes a pack of cigarettes other than the brand you or your partner usually smokes or, better still, a butt or two (with or without lipstick, depending once again on who's cheating whom) in the ashtray.

Want to make someone else's partner suspicious? If your target's male, a discreet smear of lipstick on the telephone receiver just before he goes home for the evening will transfer rather less discreetly to his jaw and/or collar—a nice way to ensure he really gets stick from his partner.

A more complex way to create doubts in someone's mind is to write off to a dating agency or, better still, a foreign marriage agency—you know the type: "Beautiful Asian girls seeking European husbands". Get the names of a few women, write them appropriately keen letters in your target's name, and leave the rest to Royal Mail and your target's partner. You may have to pay—but not nearly as dearly as your target will.

DRIVEN TO IT

Cars are an ideal place to leave incriminating notes. For maximum effect, slip a suitably salacious one— something along the lines of " . . . seeing your car brought back such delicious memories that I couldn't resist saying hello. Remember how we misted up the windows? Can't wait to see you again . . . "—under the passenger-side windscreen wiper when you know your target will be using the car with his partner.

If you can get into the car, so much the better. Tuck a passion-laden note under the sun visor so it falls out when it's pulled down. Word it carefully enough and you won't have to worry whether your target or his partner finds it—either will be made suitably suspicious by the discovery.

The sun visor is also an ideal "hiding" place for all sorts of revealing evidence. Tuck a packet of condoms (the kinkier the style the better) up there, an earring or other item of jewellery, perhaps, even a pair of (worn) knickers. The kind of calling cards prostitutes leave in phone boxes and/or a hotel receipt will cause no end of repercussions. Even something as innocent as a lighter or part-smoked packet of cigarettes (a different brand, naturally, to those either the target or his partner normally smokes) can be enough to spark a blazing row.

FAIR GAME

Prostitutes get a hard time at the hands of the law in Britain—and even ordinary, innocent women can find themselves branded common prostitutes in police records if they happen to be in the wrong area at the wrong time or some concerned citizen happens to get their information wrong and reports entirely honest comings and goings as something altogether more sleazy. Get the picture? Tell the police your ex-girl-friend or the new girl-friend of your ex-partner is on the game (use a secondary target's name when you file the complaint, of course) and watch them cop it.

COURTING DISASTER

Strike at the heart of your target's personal life by filing for divorce in her name. This is astonishingly easy. Do-It-Yourself divorce kits, along the lines of the money-saving home conveyancing kits are available now from W.H. Smith, but if you really want to make things look official, see a solicitor. You'll have to pay, but you might be able to get away with sending the bill to your target, as they rarely ask for identification.

They will ask to see your marriage certificate, but it's an easy matter to say you've lost it, the other partner has it, or that you had to leave the marital home in such a hurry there was no time for you to find it. Try to find out when and where your target was married—although the solicitor probably won't even raise an eyebrow if you say you can't quite remember—they're used to forgetful husbands and wives.

The added bonus of going through a solicitor is that the the papers will be served on your target's spouse in person. Make sure you do your homework and know where and when the solicitor will be able to reach him—and remember, it's super distressing and embarrassing for this kind of thing to happen to a person at work. Try timing the hit for when your real target—his spouse—is away on a business trip.

KEEP IT IN THE FAMILY

This scam is a particularly nasty way of causing trouble for young women, but for it to work you'll need an accomplished—and recently pregnant—young accomplice. The idea is to send your friend, who will use your target's name and address, for a pregnancy test at a Family Planning Clinic where she is not known. Naturally, the result will be positive, but when she is told the happy news, your accomplice should look scared and blurt out that the pregnancy is the result of incest with her father. Get her to plead for help. From there, hopefully, the appropriate authorities will be alerted and it won't be too long before your little scheme gestates into full-scale family embarrassment and anger.

ABORTIVE PLANS

Pregnancy arouses strong emotions, so why not use that to your benefit? Send for abortion advice in the name of your newly—and happily—pregnant target (or your target's partner). Remember, you are not in the game of being nice.

This ruse works equally well on nonpregnant targets, especially if they are young and living at home where their mail is likely to be intercepted.

Or make sure the seed of suspicion falls on fertile ground and address the information to your target's parents.

Feeling cut up over a teen romance, chaps? Get even with your ex-girl-friend and her new boyfriend at the same time by writing a letter in the latter's name to the ex's parents. Tell them she's pregnant but wants an abortion. Ask them to plead with her not to, and be sure to include the new boyfriend's phone number.

Girls can play the game, too. Simply pretend to be the new girl-friend, and write to your ex-boyfriend's folks saying you're pregnant and their irresponsible son is pressuring you to have an abortion. Either way, by the time your targets' respective parents are through with them, they'll probably both wish they'd never been born.

A twist on this tale—if your target is young and male—is to purloin the appropriate university or school letterheads and, posing as the dean or head, write a letter to your target's parents telling them that he has got a younger girl pregnant. Ask the parents to come to a meeting the following Monday and post the letter so it arrives on the Saturday morning, giving them plenty of time to stew over it. Even better, time it for when the young "dad-to-be" is away for the weekend, so there's no chance of their finding out whether it's a hoax or not for at least 24 hours.

COURTING COUPLES

Another one for teenagers: send a letter to the parents of your ex-girl-friend/boy-friend from a local solicitor. State in it that you were called down to the police station late one night (name a date when you know the target was out late) where the target and his/her partner (the new one) were being held on suspicion of pimping/prostitution/drug dealing or whatever crime takes your fancy. State that the fee of £200 for securing their release is still owing to you and that you were unimpressed by the target giving you a false address.

CARD TRICKS

Masters of revenge are always prepared. They arm themselves with information long before they need it—or they find ways of acquiring it fast when they do. So, when a relationship has outlived its usefulness and your partner has begun behaving dishonourably, it's time to make him realise that, in the game of love, the cards are stacked against him—his credit cards, to be exact, the numbers and details of which you have already had the foresight to note down.

This simple, expedient measure means you can hit him where it really hurts—the old hip-pocket nerve—by buying goods over the telephone using his credit card. Use your imagination: send a plump, pink leg of ham to your vegetarian ex-lover; order fetish gear for your prudish former mate; or send a set of encyclopaedias to the man who turned out to have the IQ of a dishcloth but not the usefulness.

Go for the adverts that promise speedy delivery (they're less likely to check that you are who you claim to be) and plan your method of attack—inundation or sending carefully selected items over a longer period—beforehand. Naturally, you can also use your ex-lover's card number to buy stuff for yourself. Do it judiciously and your little scam may never be spotted (how often do you check every single item on your credit-card statement?).

WEDDED BLITZ

Show your concern for your target's future happiness by arranging her wedding for her—without her knowledge. Hire the gown and suit, organise the church or registry office, the cars, flowers, cake, and reception, all in the target's name, of course. For maximum effect, do it while she is on holiday and leave her to face the music on her return.

PROPOSE A TOAST

Alternatively, hijack your female target's wedding arrangements. Posing as a catering company, write to her saying something along the lines of:

Dear Ms Target,

Congratulations! You have won the Posh Catering Company's Bride of the Year draw. Your prize is two of our magnificent traditional rich fruit four-tier wedding cakes (see enclosed leaflet), valued at £300. We understand the wedding reception is to be held at (fill in the details) and will arrange to deliver the cakes at the venue two hours beforehand. Please note

*that this prize is non- transferrable and there is
no cash alternative.*

*Again, our heartfelt congratulations. Your auto-
matic entry when you bought your dress/ring at
Posh Frocks/Rings certainly paid off!*

Sincerely,

*AN Other, Manager
Posh Catering Company*

Of course, this little ruse might be even more effective if your target has just had the misfortune to have
to cancel her wedding.

HEARTBREAK HOTEL

Wrecking other people's relationships can be
astonishingly easy. Planted professionally, the seed
of doubt will put down roots strong enough to
crack even the sturdiest of couples. Try the following techniques:

If your target travels alone a lot on business,
phone his home at a time when you know he's away
on a trip. When the target's partner answers, pose as
a hotel receptionist and say something along the
lines of: "After the two of you left here yesterday, the
cleaners found a couple of items of clothing and
we're wondering if they could be his". That magic
word "two" should be all that's needed to set the
partner who's left languishing at home thinking.

Alternatively, posing once again as the hotel receptionist, you could ask for the room key back—again, make sure you refer to the "two of you", as in, "I know the two of you left in a big hurry, but I hope you both enjoyed your stay."

WHAT A HEEL

A variation on this exercise is to actually mail an item of clothing—a slinky pair of high heels if your target's male, or a sexy pair of men's briefs if she's female. Enclose a note on hotel notepaper saying the items were found after "you and Mrs/Mr Target left the hotel".

ROOM SERVICE

Your target doesn't travel? Never mind, you can still play dirty. But this time you're going to go down-market. Naturally you will need to speak to your target's partner, so time your call appropriately. When he answers, identify yourself as the receptionist at a hotel in your nearest red-light area. Say something along the lines of "Mr Target left his coat/Filofax behind this afternoon after he left—we found this number on his/her business card in the pocket/inside. Perhaps he would like to drop by to collect it?" Brings a whole new meaning to service with a smile, doesn't it?

MAIL HORMONES

Want to cause some real embarrassment for your ex-lover? Try this scam, then. First, lightly and in soft, easily erasable pencil, address an empty envelope to yourself. Post it and, while waiting for it to be delivered, write a kinky sexual fantasy to your ex. Use a false name, naturally, or the name of a secondary target and be as explicit as you dare—threesomes, animals, golden showers, gay or lesbian sex, etc.

When the s.a.e. arrives, rub out your name and write in your ex's address in pen, with the secondary target as the return address if you like. Now, open the envelope and pop in your kinky missive. Don't re-seal it. The idea is to make it look as though your ex has opened it and read it. The next step is to "accidentally" drop this lurid letter somewhere where it will be found by prying eyes who know your target. Work, perhaps? The loos are always a good bet, as they give whoever finds the letter the chance to read it in privacy— although whether he or she can resist telling everyone else about it remains to be seen.

DATE WITH DESTINY

Lower down the embarrassment scale, but just as likely to cause titters in the office, is the following trick: phone your ex's workplace at a time when you know he'll be out. Tell whoever answers the phone that you're from the XYZ dating agency and that you're returning your target's call. Use the name of a real dating agency for authenticity's sake and wait for the news to spread like wildfire.

NO REGRETS

Posing as your target's phantom lover, write a

"Dear John/Jane" letter, saying something along the lines of, "*It was fun while it lasted—no regrets—but I can't stand the thought of breaking up a happy marriage. Please, forget about getting a divorce.*" Fold it up to make it look like it's been posted, received, and read, and slip it into your target's pocket, car, or wherever his or her spouse might conceivably find it.

Alternatively, write an angry letter, saying you have just found out that your target is married. Be as unpleasant as you wish, or adopt a suffering, injured tone. If your target always wears a wedding ring, make sure you say something along the lines of, "*Okay, so you wore a condom—it would have been safer for everybody if you'd worn your wedding ring, you bastard!*" for the male target, or, for the female target, "*You asked me to wear a condom—why didn't you wear your ring, you cheating bitch?*"

DOSE OF THEIR OWN MEDICINE

Here's another embarrassing ploy, with the added bonus of causing health problems for your ex's new relationship. Go to your local Family Planning or Sexually Transmitted Diseases Clinic and pick up some literature on syphilis, gonorrhoea, chlamydia, or herpes. Now get an empty pill bottle from the chemist, or one of those small envelopes pills are sometimes dispensed in, and a sticky label. Put your target's name on the label, along with last week's date, and scrawl an appropriately doctorlike instruction such as "2 tabs daily with food". Stick it to the bottle or envelope and put a couple of plain aspirin, artificial sweetener tablets, or those tiny white homoeopathic pills inside. Now plant the "evidence" someplace where your target's partner is likely to find it. Guaranteed to make your target feel lovesick.

GIVE THEM THE BRUSH-OFF

On the subject of health, here's a scam that was related to us by some friends who found themselves the butt of the joke. On holiday, they returned one evening to find that their camper van had been broken into. Nothing had been taken, so they assumed they'd just been lucky and that the thieves had been disturbed. Three weeks later when they got home they had their holiday snaps developed. Among the lovely landscapes and grinning mug shots was one photo they definitely had not taken. It showed two unfamiliar bottoms with sickeningly familiar toothbrush handles—not heads—protruding from between each pair of hairy cheeks. Now does that give you some ideas of how to get back at that arsehole who used to be your one and only?

RETURN THE RING

Has your partner given you marching orders? Here's a nice way to make her pay. Hopefully while you're clearing out your stuff, she'll clear off, too. Dial international directory enquiries (153) and ask for the number of the talking clock in some far-flung country (Australia, or New Zealand, say). Dial the number and leave the phone connected while you gather your possessions. When you leave you have two choices. You can either replace the handset or leave it off—it's up to you, although, assuming your ex's bill isn't itemised, replacing the receiver has the advantage that your target won't know the reason for her vastly inflated bill. Who said she shouldn't be let off the hook?

WAGES OF SIN

So, your partner has found somebody new and wants to wrap up the residue of your life together as quickly as possible. Take a tip from the sassy Californian woman who opted to be reasonable up to a point. Instructed by her ex-lover to sell all their joint possessions—including his beloved Porsche—with a view to splitting the proceeds, she complied. The work done, she presented him with a cheque and itemised receipt of everything sold. She had got a reasonable price for everything except the Porsche, which she sold for a knockdown $75. Okay, so she didn't get half its true worth but, when Porsche comes to shove, she got a whole lot more in terms of satisfaction.

GRAVE DOUBTS

It's sad but true—sometimes you have to go to your cheating partner's loved ones to get your own back. And if your ex's nearest and dearest are no longer living, so much the better, because graves offer a host of ways to upset your target. Try leaving fresh flowers just before she visits, or, if you're really nasty, something dead—a run-over cat or hedgehog, perhaps, skinned and dissected. Add a half-burnt candle and a knife and let her imagination do the rest. Or get some animal blood from a butcher (you love making black pudding, don't you?) and splatter the grave with it. Sounds awful? Remember, that's the idea.

BOTTLE IT UP

Here's a nice way of getting back at the lover who jumped ship. Write down all the incriminating, embarrassing, or downright false information you can think of about your ex-lover. Add your target's name, address, and phone number, then fold your note up and slip it inside a bottle. Cork it up or screw on the cap and plant it amid the morning jetsam on the shore of your nearest lake or beach or river.

An alternative is to make up a dozen or more suitably scientific-looking forms, slip them inside bottles, and plant the bottles in various locations. Include a note saying you are studying current patterns, and ask the finder to deliver the bottle and form to the target's address. Offer an incentive—say £20—for every bottle delivered, and wait for the distress signals.

PUBLISH AND BE DAMNED

Of course, if you are of a more literary bent, you could always follow the novel example of one Maureen O'Donoghue. Her foray into writing began when she daubed the words "bastard" and "bitch" on the house of her adulterous husband and his mistress. From those humble beginnings, her novel, *The Truth in the Mirror*, about women with unfaithful husbands, was born. A case of two wrongs making a writer, you might say.

SIREN'S SONG

Give your newly blissfully-in-love ex something to really feel sick about. Phone her office and leave a message saying her new partner has been involved in an accident and is seriously injured. Give the name of a hospital some distance away.

EMOTIONAL BAGGAGE

Never underestimate the strength of superglue when applied toward making you feel better. Try applying it to the locks of your soon-to-be-ex-partner's baggage before, but preferably after, he packs to leave you. If you really want to state your case, try smearing one side of his bag with glue and then sticking it to either his favourite item—the video, perhaps, or the television screen. Stick down the VCR door, with his favourite tape in for good measure, or glue up the TV remote control.

Make your partner realise the relationship has gone down the drain by adding a glop or two to plugs—pressed down firmly in the plug hole, of course—or to electrical plugs in their sockets. Show you take a dim view by gluing the dimmer switches in the minimum position, or go for a time-delay effect by gluing electric light bulbs in their sockets. Ensure he never plays "your" song for some new love by gluing favourite records inside their sleeves and tapes and CDs inside their cases.

Make him remember your promise to stick together by sticking book and photo album pages together, tinned food to the shelf, and cups and saucers to one another or the table. Leave him with hang-ups: glue the telephone handset to the cradle, and make sure he has no chance of getting a parting shot by gluing the lids on the scotch, gin, and brandy bottles. Really piss him off by gluing down the toilet seat and lid. Then, as you leave, shut him up for good by applying a generous amount of glue to all external locks.

VINTAGE STUFF

The last word when it comes to treating that philandering partner to a taste of revenge has to go to Britain's most famous mistress of the art in recent years, Lady Sarah Graham-Moon. As well as hacking an arm off each of her errant husband's Savile Row suits and pouring six litres of white paint over his beloved BMW, her master stroke of revenge was to hit him where it really hurt—down below. In his cellar to be precise. Sir Peter's cellar, you see, was home to a particularly fine collection of expensive vintage wines, such as Chateau Latour claret—and it was his pride and joy.

Lady Graham-Moon decided to share his good taste with the residents in the village where Sir Peter's mistress lived, so she lugged the bottles upstairs, loaded up her car with them, then drove off on a delivery run, leaving a bottle of the very best on every resident's doorstep next to their morning pinta. Proof indeed that hell hath no fury like a woman scorned. Cheers, Lady Graham-Moon.

Restaurants
and Shops

*B*rittain has long been known as a nation of shopkeepers, but it wasn't until the eighties that we truly became a nation of shoppers, embracing the credit-card culture of our American cousins with an enthusiasm that has ensured many of us are still paying them off 10 years later. And, despite the huge sums of money we are still spending in these recessionary times, the service we get in many restaurants and shops still comes with more of a sneer than a smile. Don't take it lying down. Remind these rude souls that the customer is always right and return their service with balls.

RESTAURANTS

Don't you just hate it when you go out to an expensive restaurant, spend half the evening trying to attract the attention of a supercilious waiter, get told off when you attempt to pour your own wine, and then get presented with a hefty 17 percent service charge at the end of it all? Of course, the first thing you can do, if the charge is marked on the menu as "optional", is to take up the option of not paying it. But sometimes it's just not convenient to make your scene at the time—maybe you're with business associates, on a date, or taking your granny out for a treat. Stay calm; bear in mind that revenge is a dish best eaten cold, and serve up your retribution in the bitterest of sauces . . .

Caught in a Trap

Take along a matchbox containing a couple of the biggest, swiftest, meanest-looking cockroaches you can find. Just before the end of your meal, surreptitiously release them and hope they run away from you rather than up your leg. With luck, someone else will raise the alarm, taking the suspicion off you. But if the rest of the diners are an unobservant lot, you'll have to draw on your own talent as an actor or actress. Point, shriek, gag, and say you feel ill. Mention the health authorities. With any luck you'll get away without having to pay the bill.

No live cockroaches? Well, substitute the next best thing—a dead one. Order a nice, gooey, chocolatey pudding and get stuck in, but, no matter how good it is, don't finish it. Instead, drop your trusty dead friend in the bowl and partly cover him with the sauce and a glob of pudding. Once again, gasp, gag, and get your companion to call over the waiter. Make sure everyone else who is dining there hears what you've just found in your pudding— and that, worse, you've just eaten half of it. Retch and race off to the loo, napkin to your mouth.

Guaranteed to make those greedy restaurateurs feel ill.

No monster cockies? Try emptying a bag of dried dog turds under the table. "Accidentally" kick one out from under the table into the path of either a fellow patron or waiter and wait for the shit to hit the fan.

A variation on this theme is to bring a mouse into the restaurant and liberate it at some time during the meal. If you are planning to pick one up at the pet shop, choose a brown, grey, or black one—an obviously tame white mouse will give rise to suspicion. Then let him go at a suitable moment and watch your restaurateur squirm as he explains the presence of vermin on his premises. Hard cheese, as they say.

Lettuce Prey

Restaurants with help-yourself salad bars and carverys are almost too easy. Think of the endless opportunities here for sweet—and sour—revenge. On a very simple level you can "season" dishes with extra salt, sugar, minced dried garlic, cayenne pepper, or curry powder. But if this still seems a little too lukewarm, serve up something more spectacular. Your cockroach might like to make a guest appearance in the Thousand Island dressing, a deceased mouse could pop up in the cottage cheese, live maggots would probably appreciate being rehoused among the cold chicken wings, and a big, fat slug would be an authentic-looking addition to the lettuce display.

Baby, Don't Go

If your annoyance with the restaurant is relatively

mild, you might like to suggest it as a venue next time you go out with your friends and their young offspring. Teething babies can quite often scream for a whole evening. It's no skin off your nose—you'd have been stuck listening to it anyway—but it can really irritate customers visiting the restaurant for business or romantic purposes. Similarly, a toddler who's at that "into everything" age can wreak havoc with a dessert trolley but is a little too young to be thrown out by the scruff of the neck. Even the snottiest maitre d' is expected to suffer little children.

Helpings for the Homeless

Sometimes it's possible to get your revenge while helping out a good cause at the same time. Think of the satisfaction of knowing you're helping the homeless to a good meal and settling a score with a restaurateur who's done you wrong. Take a stroll around your local Skid Row and pick up 10 odoriferous tramps in need of a good meal. Bring them along to your targeted buffet restaurant, settle them down, and order a plate for each.

At this point, one of two things will happen. Either the waiter will just take the order and you can sit back and watch your aromatic new friends empty that restaurant and salad bar simultaneously, or the waiter will alert the manager, who will attempt to eject you and your pals. He will, of course, be quite within his rights to do this—legally. Morally, though, it doesn't look good to throw out starving people, especially if a generous soul such as yourself is willing to pay for them. Tell him you'll be mentioning this to the local—or maybe a national —newspaper, and that you'll be writing to Shelter and contacting Anita Roddick.

You probably won't have to, though. A crowd of hungry street people that has just been offered, and then refused, an all-you-can-eat slap-up meal is liable to behave antisocially. Your manager may well decide to just cut his losses and come to some other arrangement with you all.

Get Stuffed

Make your target put his money where your mouth is. Place an advert in the local press with a cut-out coupon offering two meals for the price of one, plus a free bottle of wine on presentation of the coupon. Make up your own artwork on a home computer using the logo of the restaurant to add a touch of authenticity. Pay cash if necessary when you deliver, and don't hang around to chat. Your target will soon have an excited stream of customers who are soon to be irritated ex-customers, or, to keep the peace, he'll have to subsidise all those cut-price meals which, as you forgot to put an expiry date on the coupon, could keep coming for quite a while. Oh, and he'll probably lose his temper with the local paper, which could also be bad for business.

Off the Menu

Get back at the restaurant that serves up rubbish by giving it a helping hand with its menu. You can do this in two ways. You could type up a menu very like the restaurant's own, listing the usual dishes, but at prices so inflated even your target rip-off restaurateurs wouldn't get away with it, or at prices so low they'd send them broke. Alternatively, you could list dishes that are calculated to offend even the most adventurous palate. Try Dog Sausages, Baked Rat Entrails, or Sheep's Eye Paté. If you want to be more subtle—and the restaurant serves Continental cuisine—translate the above stomach-turners into French.

Now, either pay a visit to your target eatery and remove the loose menus from their covers and substitute your own, or, even better if you can find a way to do it, gain access to the glass menu display box many restaurants have on their outside walls and slip your improved menu in in place of the real thing.

Failing that, a sign pasted over the display box saying "Closed for private party" can do terrible things to the restaurant's takings, as can adverts announcing "Closed for refurbishment" placed judiciously in the local press.

Hep, Hep, Hurray

You can also keep customers away in droves by printing an official-looking Department of Health mailshot asking people to submit evidence for an enquiry into your target restaurant:

To the Householder,

It has been brought to our attention that several people have developed infectious hepatitis after eating at (restaurant's name). If you have visited this restaurant in the past two months, we would strongly urge you to attend your nearest hospital's infectious diseases clinic for a blood test. If you have contracted hepatitis, we ask that you inform us, as this will help with our case. Should the prosecution be successful, you will naturally be eligible for compensation. All replies will be held in strictest confidence.

Yours sincerely,

AN Other
Chief Hygiene Officer

Take the usual precautions of using a plausibly official return address, i.e., the right building and street for the local Department of Health, but a fictitious department and name. Now, if that doesn't have your target restaurateur feeling liverish, I don't know what will.

Road to Run

Another way to get the health inspector interested in them is to plant animal parts in their rubbish bins. Find a freshly killed dog or cat corpse, skin it, remove the head, legs, and viscera, bag them, and leave them in your target's rubbish. Dump the corpse elsewhere. Now, before their rubbish is removed, alert the health authorities—anonymously, of course—to the "fact" that the restaurant is using cat and dog meat. As they say, there's many ways to skin a cat . . .

Condoments

Good chefs will tell you that the key to good cooking is careful spicing, and that means a judicious hand with the condiments. But if your target is a cafeteria or self-service buffet where the chef was obviously not listening all through his catering course, perhaps you need to teach him a lesson he won't forget in a hurry by perking up the food with something a little more, er, spicy, than mere salt and pepper. A condom, to be exact.

Next time you're at your target venue, have handy a condom. Wait for a lull around the soup tureen, remove the condom from its wrapper, and drop it in the pot. You may find it less obvious to drop it in your bowl, then simply touch the ladle to it—it should stick. Replace the ladle in the tureen and remove yourself to a table from where you will have a good view of the action when the condom is ladled up by the next customer. Not so much French cuisine as Frenchie cuisine.

Condoms can also be secreted in the salad bar— under the potato salad, perhaps, or something equally gooey. Squirt a little mayonnaise inside the condom before adding it, for that truly authentic touch. Now that's what we'd call real self-service.

Fowl Play

This will work for many businesses but is particularly suited to restaurants, which are sensitive to unpleasant odours. Acquire four or five chickens— dead ones. Quality is unimportant here, as the recipe requires that they are given plenty of time to mature. Toss them onto the roof of your target's restaurant. If you can actually get up there, you might like to post portions down the chimney as well. As passers-by are often lured into a restaurant by the aroma outside, you can imagine the effect this finger-lickin' chicken recipe will have on business.

Toilet Humour

While we're playing chicken, you might introduce your featherless friends to your establishment's lavatories. A mature piece of raw chicken or fish inside the paper towel dispenser will introduce a little dry humour.

You can block the toilets by soaking several sponges in a thick starch solution, binding them small and tight with string and then, when they're dry, unbinding the string and flushing them down the loo. With luck, the sponges will get quite some way down the pipe before they start to expand, leaving your targeted restaurateur in deep, er, trouble.

For those with money to spend on malice, you could have a set of official-looking stickers printed up from the local "health authority". Include a logo, a signature, and a message along the lines of: *"DANGER: THESE TOILETS ARE CLOSED DUE TO INFECTIOUS VENEREAL DISEASE. STAY OUT FOR YOUR OWN HEALTH PROTECTION."*

If you want to hit a target by embarrassing his clients, try doctoring the urinals. Target the kind with built-in washer pipes that discharge periodically to clean out the urinals. Turn off the main tap, then rotate the sections of pipe containing the jets until they point upward, toward the urinal user. Needless to say, next time the urinals are flushed, your manager will be faced with a group of damp and flushed-looking male customers demanding an explanation.

SHOPS

Supermarkets are among the few businesses in this country to have come out of this recession ahead. Unlike everyone else, profits are booming and the largest three, Sainsbury's, Safeway, and Tesco, are reported to have got together in a legal and public relations campaign in an attempt to stop an American food discount store from entering the British market. The high profit margins of British supermarkets compared with those in Europe and the US are legendary—as are our stores' talents for keeping competitors out of the way. Unfortunately, we all have to eat, so this stranglehold on food is especially hard to swallow.

Thin Ice

Whatever your gripe, give them a taste of their own medicine. You could start by loading up a trolley with a large selection of frozen goods. Premium ice cream, frozen salmon, gateaux, and those expensive ready-meals can warm up pretty quickly on a hot day, and if you can leave them in a quiet corner, it could be hours before your damp rejects are discovered.

An old-fashioned cardboard box of ice cream left behind a display of cereals or bread will leave them with a sticky situation, as will rigging a stack of egg cartons so they fall over. A small hole in a carton of milk or orange juice will spread your influence quickly, and a discreet cut in a box or bag of soap powder will create that whiter-than-white look all over the floor.

Rather than waste items within the store, you

may prefer to introduce goodies of your own. A trip to a fisherman's bait shop will furnish you with enough maggots to close down the entire high street. A little "nest" of them found on a piece of steak will have most red-blooded males running for the quiche section—until they notice that the ingredient they thought was a piece of mushroom is actually moving, too . . .

Chair of Gloom

Furniture is so expensive, it's only fair to expect some cooperation from the store if there's a problem. Sometimes, though, you go through all the right channels and find that, due to small print, you're stuck with the sofa that turned out to be a completely different colour from the one in the brochure, or the chair that's so badly designed it leaves you feeling as though a small herd of rhino have just wiped their feet on your back.

It's at times like this that you need to put the store in the hot seat. Pop in with your trusty penknife and make a couple of nice, long slashes along the side of a sofa or chair, or fill a fountain pen with ink and be a little careless with it near an expensive, cream-coloured suite. A water pistol filled with bleach can also leave an interesting design behind. For best results, time your visit to coincide with the start of a sale or major in-store promotion.

Sound Advice

If you want to sound off at a record store, here's how to hit the right note. Offer a little free publicity. Advertise that a particular band is going to be making a guest appearance at the store to promote its record. Imagine the disturbance that could be caused by hundreds of disappointed teenage girls who have been waiting outside a store since 7 A.M. for Take That. And one can only speculate about the reaction of a crowd of Motorhead fans to being made to look stupid by a greedy, deceitful record store. Music lovers can certainly be an unpredictable lot.

Good as Gold

Ever been conned into buying a "solid gold" chain or ring that turned out to be gold plate? Don't waste time getting in a row over it. Revisit your cheap jeweller under the guise of being so delighted with your purchase that you want to buy lots more. Then, when all the items are in front of you, get out your handy, lidded container of potassium iodide, inform the jeweller that, just to be on the safe side, you are going to check the items are all solid gold—and start dropping them in. Potassium iodide will strip gold plate, but solid gold, naturally, is perfectly safe. With luck, you will find you have been offered a refund before you are forced to finish your experiment by testing the rest of the merchandise.

Piss Them Off

Just how angry *are* you with this shop? If you're really pissed off—and male—you could try venting your spleen via your bladder. This one involves using a catheter and attaching a length of flexible tubing to run down your leg under your trousers and down through an old shoe. You can imagine the rest. You just pay a visit to the shop that took the piss—and return the compliment. Have plenty to drink before you set off and make sure you keep still while you're doing it. Aim to make several return visits—enough to leave that charming Piccadilly urinal smell in the air and necessitate an expensive change of carpet. This works best in expensively fitted-out shops with plenty of snobby customers who will be sure to kick up a stink.

Salespeople

Finally, there are the shopkeepers who come to your door—door-to-door salesmen who pester you in your own home, whose only overheads are their shoe leather and the electricity bill that you pay, and who, unless you're prepared to be very rude indeed, have been trained not to take no for an answer. Double-glazing salesmen used to be the worst, but they've mostly taken refuge at the end of the phone, from where one can only assume they understand even less about your double glazing requirements.

Brush sellers, insurance salesmen, and the ency-clopaedia bunch still do the rounds, but, speaking for ourselves, the kind of salesman we receive most regu-larly is the kind selling me eternal life, rather than life insurance. Unfortunately, those who believe they're on speaking terms with God have an unstoppable belief that they know better than you what's good for you. They are like mothers-in-law from hell. Here's how to deal with them:

- Appear to be interested in what they have to say, then start asking kinky personal questions.
- Fall down on your knees and start praying.

- Act perfectly normally, except for persistently scratching your genitals. When you notice them looking, apologise and tell them it's your crabs.
- Come to the door stark naked. If that doesn't faze them, invite them in to discuss your New Age beliefs, such as the laying on of hands.
- Come to the door in a devil's costume and mask.

Take Your Time

This is for those of you who have received one of those letters from a time-share company informing you that you've definitely won a prize and all you have to do is come along and listen to an hour-long sales spiel about the joys of time-share living. Anyone who's experienced this will tell you that it's high-pressure selling at its worst, so bad, in fact, that the law was changed to allow people a legal opt-out for several days after signing time-share papers.

Salesmen of this sort deserve everything they get, so if you're going to spend your precious time listening to them in order to get your "prize", take up a little of their time in return. Tell them you want to buy three time-shares, haggle a little, ask for a discount. Hem and haw about the locations you want, and ask a lot of tedious questions. Get them to phone you at home and go on about how you need to talk to your bank manager. In the end, when you've agreed to everything, the papers are all drawn up and you're ready to sign, say, "Oh, I was only kidding", and walk away.

Take All of the Credit

Target a bit of a shopaholic? Can't make it through

to the end of the month without without some help from her flexible friend? If revenge is on the cards, help relieve her of this unhealthy addiction by cancelling her credit cards for her. This is very easy to do—it has to be. All you need to know is what kind of credit cards your target has. All the main credit-card companies have emergency lines and will cancel a "stolen" card if you can provide just a name and address, although having the number simplifies things considerably. Be sure, however, that you know exactly what card it is. For example, Barclaycard and Girobank Visa are both Visa cards, but they are operated by different companies and have separate emergency numbers. The operator is likely to get just a little suspicious if you can't remember which one "you" hold.

Alternatively, you might like to render them useless by erasing the information on the brown magnetic strip at the back using a bulk-tape eraser—used to erase information from floppy disks and available from computer stockists. This will mean the card registers as void if used in a cashpoint machine or "wiped" through an electronic checkout. However, for sheer embarrassment value, simply reporting the card stolen is probably your best course of action.

Of course, if you've got your target's credit-card details, you might like to do a little shopping on his or her behalf before actually cancelling the cards. You'll need to know the name on the card, the number, expiry date, and address to which bills are sent. This isn't stealing, of course, because you'll be buying it all for your target. Think of it all as a farewell present, as you order a wide selection of goodies, from sex aids to one-way tickets to Sydney.

If it's an ex-lover, you might like to spread your largesse to the spouse with a big bouquet from your ex bearing the message, "Sorry I've been unfaithful to you for the past three years. Let's start again, darling". Do all your shopping in one hit so that your target doesn't have a chance to cancel the card. Regard it as redistributive plastic surgery and be satisfied that financial cuts are always among the most painful.

Sex

*E*nlarge your enemy's family for him. If wifey is a school-days or university sweetheart, imagine what a surprise it would be for him to receive a "Happy Birthday, Daddy" card from out of town, especially if the return address were that of a long-lost classmate. Make that address just slightly illegible so the mystery can't be cleared up, and continue to spread a little happiness at Christmas and on Father's Day. Threaten a surprise visit if you're feeling particularly malicious.

SEXUAL HANG-UP

Having problems with an obscene caller? If the creep wants to meet you, play along with him and arrange to meet him in a bar in a couple of hours. Afterwards, invite the police to your get-together . . .

HEALTH HAZARDS

The advent of the personal computer has done

wonders for the world of justice and retribution. An AppleMac or similar model can produce official-looking forms and letterheads for all occasions, like, for example, that of a clinic for sexually transmitted diseases. Everybody loves getting letters, so make your unfaithful lover's day by dropping her a line to the effect that she has been sexually active with a partner who has been diagnosed HIV-positive and that she should refrain from sexual relations of any kind until their case can be diagnosed. Instruct her to bring this letter to the above address at a set date and time (add some case numbers and reference numbers in Biro to give it an "official" look), and insist that she bring along any spouse or regular sexual partner. This can be particularly revealing if you are the wronged spouse.

If your target is particularly gullible, you can have the fun of watching her give herself a "positive" HIV test with your own special do-it-yourself home testing kit. If the target hasn't actually been participating in any extra-curricular sexual activity, state that there have been suspected incidents of people possibly contracting the disease from fleas. With the letter you have enclosed, wrapped in wax paper, several test strips you have made yourself by soaking blotting paper in a strong cobalt-chloride solution and drying it thoroughly. Stamp each strip with "control numbers" to give it an authentic touch. Your target should be instructed to dip a strip into a sample of her urine—a change in colour from white or light pink to strong blue or purple will indicate a positive result and, in this instance, will mean that all sexual partners should take the test, too. The strips should then be returned to the "issuing agency"—a bogus room number at the local health authority. Supply a stamped, preprinted return envelope to add authenticity. Of course, any moisture will turn cobalt chloride blue.

If your target is particularly sleazy, with a wide circle of sexual acquaintances, you could arrange to have the local "health authority" call him or her direct. A call from a busy and authoritative Dr Smith informing the target that her name has appeared on a list supplied to the health authority by one of its genital herpes patients will certainly get her attention. Make the call at her office, and you should get everybody else's attention, too. Brush aside all denials, and ask specific, embarrassing questions about what, when, and with whom. Ask for the names and addresses of all sexual partners for the past six months, and advise her to make an appointment with her doctor for immediate tests. Keep a copy of the health authority's phone number in case your target wants to verify the call—can you imagine trying to trace a Dr Smith in that bureaucratic nightmare?

Alternatively, make a telephone call to your target's home when you know he or she will be out but his or her other half will be in. In your most breezy, official-sounding manner, identify yourself as a doctor at the local clinic and ask to speak to your target— we'll call him Mr Target, although this one works equally well for women. When told he's not at home, affect concern, hem and haw a bit, and then come out with "the truth".

"You are Mrs Target? I am so sorry to have to tell you in this way, but as the matter concerns you, too, I am obliged to let you know . . . "

The thrust of the good doctor's message is that Mr Target's AIDS and genital herpes tests are "generally negative", but that the clinic still needs to talk to him about the woman with whom he was involved, because they have reason to believe she is a carrier. If Mr Target is one of those married men who complains that he and his wife have nothing to talk about anymore, you will probably have opened up those lines of communication faster than any marriage-guidance counsellor ever could.

HOT SHOTS

It can be painful when a love affair dies, but if you suspect your pain is greater than your ex's, console yourself with a flick through the old photo album and pick out shots of happier times—especially any fun ones that you took of him or her in, er, bed. Get a few prints made—about 50—and share that happiness with your ex's colleagues. Under the windscreen wipers in the office carpark is a good distribution point.

SUSPICIOUS MINDS

If your target is a man, arrange for a female voice to call his home and ask for him by name, or by a pet name—either made up or used only by his wife. If his wife answers, hang up as soon as she starts asking questions. Phone back half an hour later and hang up as soon as she answers the phone. Repeat three more times, then leave Mrs Target to draw her own conclusions.

Alternatively, call the target's home during the day, posing as his concerned employer and asking where he is. When your target's wife expresses her belief that he is at work, the "employer" should affect embarrassment, hem and haw a bit, and then, as if prompted by somebody else, say something like, "Oh yes, I'm terribly sorry to have bothered you. He is here, after all. Er, thank you." For best results, this trick should be performed when your target really is out of the office on genuine business so that when Mrs Target phones back to talk to him, he won't be there.

BABY LOVE

Spread your target's reputation. Create a chain letter and send it to any members of the Moral Majority who spring to mind. Here's the wording:

Hi, Swinger!

We were given your name by some local friends as someone who would love to share in our kiddie-porn chain letter. We've enclosed a censored-version sample of the kind of fun we have in mind. Since we've been told that you also have some of the stuff our members want to see, all you have to do is send some prints of the real thing to the top name on the list. Then retype the list, removing the top name and adding your own to the bottom. Quickly, your name will move to the top of the list and you'll receive thousands of photos of young boys and girls in

juicy poses. Join in the fun—send your photos
today to the top name on the list.

No prizes for guessing whose name and address will appear at the top of the list. An innocent snapshot of a very young child at the seaside or swimming pool should be enclosed—though not a child of your personal acquaintance. Resist the temptation to fill the list with names and addresses of other enemies—you do not want too many trails to lead back to you—and before you can say Esther Rantzen, your target will be explaining his idiosyncratic epistles to the boys in blue.

ON THE JOB

For some unknown reason, there's a certain type of middle management suit who thinks that any woman employed in his department becomes his sexual property. The trouble is, confronting creeps of this kind often lands you in more trouble than it does him. The answer, naturally, is to land him in so much trouble with *his* boss that he won't ever be in a position to trouble *you* again. Acquire a copy of the creep in question's CV—secretaries are usually in a good position to get hold of this kind of thing.

Failing that, make one up based on what you do know. Then apply for lots of new jobs in your target's name. Make sure the companies are all in the same area of business—preferably close competitors. Your covering letter should give clear reasons as to why "you" want to move. Here are a few suggestions: your boss won't stop making homosexual advances toward you; the company is dropping standards to save cash and is rapidly going out of business; you suspect the chairman of fraud and want to get out before the big crash. Bad news travels fast, especially when it's about a business competitor, and it shouldn't be long before your man is enjoying some intense intercourse with *his* boss.

CREAM TEASE

Want to hit him where it really hurts? It lacks subtlety, but a get-well-soon card and a tube of penis enlarger cream (see the small ads in smutty magazines or the *Sunday Sport*) will hit the spot.

Sometimes subtlety is wasted on the unfaithful swine, anyway. If your man is doing you wrong, why not just send him a condom filled with mayonnaise and the message, "You forgot this last night."

"Used" condoms also make a witty addition to you target's doorstep or front garden—especially if he or she has young children. Kiddies have a tireless thirst for knowledge, and chances are, they'll be first to find your gift and will rush in to ask Mummy or Daddy, "What's this for, please?"

HOTEL HELL

If your enemy is regularly entertaining a friend at a quiet hotel, let him or her know the secret's out. Get access to a computer, dummy up your very own Hideaway Hotel Frequent Customer Club, and invite your target to join. Send it to whichever address is most likely to offer an audience come opening time.

If your target has a secretary who screens all his calls, you can turn it to your advantage in this variation. Phone your target's office and, when asked the inevitable questions about your business, drop your voice and answer conspiratorially, "It's rather personal. You see, I'm the cleaning lady over at the Painted Lady Club, and I found one of Mr Target's credit cards by one of the beds. I just wanted to get it back to him." Your target will have a reputation as a bit of a card himself just as soon as that secretary can get off the phone.

You might also phone and make reservations for your target at a smart out-of-town hotel. Give the home number and ask for confirmation two days before the reservation date. Or call a travel agency and book trips for two on your target's behalf—only substitute his wife's name for that of his secretary or another woman and insist on that itinerary being sent to his home.

BLOW HIS COVER

If your target likes to go for long walks, complain to the local school that you have seen him "flashing" children. Give a detailed description, including the clothing he usually wears, and site the "offence" very close to where he lives. Your target will soon find himself in for some very unpleasant exposure indeed.

WILLY WARMER

Unfaithful pricks are the worst. Not only do they break your heart, they also put your health at serious risk. Remind him of the discomfort of social diseases, and practice your own form of safe sex. Next time he wants to get it on, start off by giving him a long, slow helping hand—and spice things up with your own lubricant additive. Travellers may have brought back a jar of Tiger Balm, the miracle Eastern cure-all, which is guaranteed to bring a powerful warmth to his loins. Alternatively, Deep Heat ointment is sure to make him really hot . . .

Alternatively, if you feel able to make yourself even more intimate with the creep, bear in mind that certain substances cause only mild discomfort when held in the mouth but absolute agony when applied to the nether regions. Mustard and Tabasco sauce could be just the things you need to spice up that final farewell. Rest assured that by the time you've finished, he'll be wanting to blow on his own dick.

You could go a little further if the prick in question really deserves it. Mix alcohol with superglue, and the solution won't dry until heat is applied. Use it as a lubricant in a condom, and the next pair of hands little Willy places himself in will be down at the casualty department of the local hospital.

Finally, an American woman is reported to have superglued her errant husband's tackle to his leg while he was asleep. The parting of the ways had to be stage-managed by a doctor while the lady in question completed the treatment with a large removal van at the family home. This trick is particularly recommended for men who often have erotic dreams.

MOBILE MASTURBATION

Irritated by a dork with a portable phone? The only thing that seems to have grown faster in recent years than these mobile menaces are telephone sex lines, which now provide a large chunk of the revenue for our good country's most popular national newspapers. Why not help out the poor inadequates who patronise these services by putting them in touch with a genuine, live dickhead instead of just a prerecorded fake orgasm? Those expensive 10-digit 08 numbers really are remarkably like mobile phone numbers, so mistakes are easily made.

Make him an offer he can't refuse. Something like, *"Hot and horny live sex talk. Talk your dirtiest for one minute—I promise to come right back and outdo you! Just ring my bell!!"* The bell in question is, of course, your target's mobile phone. Print up little cards—perhaps with some choice illustrative material from an appropriate magazine—and distribute around Soho telephone boxes.

EVERY PICTURE TELLS A STORY

If your target is known for being a prudish bore, help him out by getting him a really racy reputation. Acquire some pornography—the top shelf of most newsagents will do the trick unless you have something really unusual in mind, in which case try the small ads at the back of the mag. When you have found pictures to your taste, copy them onto 35mm colour film. Then send the film off for developing in your target's name.

One of several things may happen: the developer may simply develop the film and send the pictures to your target—something that will offend and outrage him greatly; the developer may, as is his right, refuse to develop the pornography and write a sniffy letter to your target telling him so; or the developer may feel that the kind of pictures sent are illegal and notify the authorities. Whatever course of action taken, your target's in for a real eye-opener.

There's another way you can use photography to embarrass your target: using composite photographs. Magazines and newspapers often use these to illustrate articles, sometimes without actually revealing that the picture is a composite. However, you do need to be pretty competent in photography and airbrushing techniques or have a trusted friend who is.

Alternatively, if you work in magazines, newspapers or graphic design, you may have access to computer technology for "blending" images. Of course, the uses for such images are limited only by your imagination. For example, a shot of your target leaving a restaurant, or maybe even a hotel, with someone of the opposite sex could create an air of tension if sent to the target's spouse, especially if accompanied by a covering note reading, "Keep that slut of a wife/sleazy husband of yours away from my man/girlfriend."

Other possibilities are to send pictures of the target in a compromising situation with someone of the same sex (get a few prints done for the office), or to send the police pictures of the target's car kerb crawling (make sure that licence plate is clearly visible). This is such a versatile idea, you have scope to really make sure the punishment fits the crime.

OUT OF ORDER

Is your target a homophobe? Broaden his mind and have a gay old time at his expense by introducing him to one of your more flamboyant friends. Pick an occasion when Mr Target will be out in public with Mrs Target and send in your pal, dressed to kill—aim for a menopausal Julian Clary look if you can manage it or, failing that, a leather-clad clone, complete with moustache and cap. Your friend should run into them "by accident" and should become angry, tearful, and, above all, *loud*.

Imagine your target's surprise when he is confronted by this screaming apparition pointing at his wife and demanding to know who the bitch is. Lines such as "I knew you were still in the closet, but I didn't know you were using a cover"; "I wondered where you got those crabs from, I can't believe you could put me at risk in this way"; and "It's her or me. Ditch the bitch or it's over!" should be delivered quickly before beating an angry and outraged retreat.

If you can't find anyone with the nerve to go through this scenario, just getting your pretty male friend to shout, "Stop looking at my dick, you creep!" will be enough to redden faces and possibly even sow seeds of doubt in the mind of his female companion.

If your target is an insecure macho male, "outing" him, as it is known on the other side of the Atlantic, is one of your most efficient tools of revenge. You could, for example, forge a shy, nervous letter from your target to his male boss or a friend declaring his passionate love. Make it really soul-searching. Explain that this feeling has been growing for some time and that "you" just "don't want to live a lie anymore".

Ask him not to reject this love out of hand—you know that he feels the same way about you, too. Throw in some pious guff about safe sex, along with a packet of heavy-duty condoms if you feel inspired. Provided you make your letter convincing, this one's a winner whatever you do. If the letter's recipient is straight, it will result in tension and probably an embarrassing meeting. If he's gay, well, who knows?

A friend once managed to "out" somebody long-distance. She had an Australian lodger called Dennis whose only topic of conversation was cricket and who would leave the flat looking slightly messier than if she had left a pot-bellied pig locked in a sitting room for three days. Dennis' proudest asset was his abundance of testosterone—a pity, considering nobody wanted any part of it—and he made Paul Hogan look like Liberace.

Our friend managed to tolerate the personal habits—he was, after all, only staying in the country for six months. It was when he finally "disappeared", owing her a large sum of money and without returning her keys, that she felt really angry. She fumed for days, as she had no forwarding address and no means of recovering her cash. Then she got a phone call from a friend of his. She realised that there was no point in appealing to this friend to get her money back. The fact that he was a friend of Dennis' made him suspect, but she didn't want him to get off the phone until her debt was repaid—psychologically if not financially.

She acted surprised and embarrassed that he'd phoned. She said that Dennis had gone off travelling with a friend, but that she didn't know where. The friend, of course, asked which friend he'd gone with. She hesitated for a minute, then said "Paolo". The friend had, of course, never heard of Paolo, and asked her who he was. She hesitated again before blurting out, "Look, I don't think being gay is anything to be ashamed of, do you? Dennis says his friends would never understand, but I think any real friend would be supportive. I'm pleased that Dennis has found love at last and doesn't have to hang around those cricket changing rooms any more. Paolo's a great guy, and I think they'll be very happy."

She even managed to persuade the friend not to tell Dennis—"He's kept it secret for years", she said, "I only found out because I was living with him"—but she feels certain he shared the information with others from Dennis' circle, and she says knowing that makes those few pounds she lost worthwhile.

PREGNANT PAUSE

Targeting a two-timing woman? Break up in

style and make her pay—literally. Arrange to go out to a top restaurant and order the most expensive items on the menu. Just after the first course arrives, leap to your feet, look her in the eye, and scream, "Pregnant? What do you mean, pregnant? You never did that with me!" Then storm out of the place, leaving her to pick up the bill and face down the spectators.

BLOW JOB

You can add a festive air to your target's car by treating him to some inflatable sex dolls—be generous, get three or four—filling them with helium gas (readily available from party-balloon sellers; check the Yellow Pages) and stuffing them into his car boot. As soon as the boot is opened, the dolls will fly off. You can add to the fun by making sure your mark is reunited with his friends.

Attach a message to each doll along the lines of: "*I belong to (target's name). If found, please return me to (address of target's office).*" Bear in mind that also offering a generous reward will greatly increase the chances of your target's pneumatic pals finding their way home, not to mention the aggravation caused when their finder demands payment.

TART RESPONSE

Looking for that extra-special surprise for your target? Employ a little professional help. A great many ladies of the night—and, indeed, gentlemen—are only too happy to make house calls, so choose a night when your target and spouse will be in and organise a hired help to liven up their evening. This works especially well if you know the birthday of the spouse. If your pro arrives singing "Happy Birthday" and announcing herself as a special surprise present, it could just about wrap up his marriage.

Social Occasions

Social embarrassment can be appallingly difficult to live down—and hardly anyone is immune to it. Remember that friend who held a party that simply failed to get going, or the meal you attended where the food was inedible and the cook was left with his reputation as a host in tatters? Remember, too, how reluctant you were to attend his next bash? Now if only you could humiliate your target so easily . . .

Nobody likes a party pooper, but sometimes it can be particularly edifying to rain on your target's parade. Destroy a dinner party with some especially revolting behaviour and your hosts may never invite you again, but you can bet the other guests will be reluctant to risk a repeat performance by dining with them again, too. On the other hand, there are more subtle ways to spoil things. After all, why ruin your social standing as well as your target's?

Here are a few ideas to help you on the road to celebrating your target's downfall.

PLAY IT AGAIN, SAM

Party walls take on extra meaning when you have inconsiderate neighbours—you know, the kind who hold regular all-night bashes with the stereo turned up full-blast and the kind of loud guests who insist on dumping their glasses and empty bottles over your side of the fence, blowing their horns as they arrive and leave, and staging full-scale slanging matches outside your door.

Then there's the party animals from the past, with their penchant for playing the long version of "Stairway to Heaven" at sound-barrier crashing volume at a quarter to three every Saturday morning; or the ones who, after two-and-half cans of Special Brew, grow terminally sentimental, haul out the guitar and amp and to give the neighbourhood their pathetic rendition of "Smoke on the Water". If they enjoy it so much, think of how appreciative they'll be to hear it all again the next day.

Wait till your targets hold the next rave, then get your tape-player and a good microphone and record a good 90 minutes of the hell-raising. Next morning, nice and early—say around 6:30, 7 o'clock—pack a picnic and head off somewhere quiet for the day—but before you go, position your tape-player against the wall of your neighbours' bedroom if you live in a flat or terraced house, or as close as possible to their home if you're in a detached area. Now load the machine with the tape you recorded the previous evening, turn the volume up full-blast, and exit swiftly. This is particularly effective if you have an auto-reverse player, as your tape, literally, will not stop.

RAISE THE ALARM

Another option, and one that can be done in all "innocence" is to "accidentally" set your clock-radio alarm to go off around two in the morning. Unless you work night shift, save this method until you're going away for the weekend or on holiday. Set the alarm so the radio comes on for, say, 15 minutes—most have an automatic cut-off period, but some allow you to determine the amount of time yourself. Tune the radio to a loud rock station, turn the volume right up, and position it against the wall.

A couple of nights of disturbed sleep should be all it takes to make your neighbours realise how annoying it is to be awoken by loud music. When confronted, affect concern and pretend to be terribly apologetic, murmuring that you are well aware how awful it is to have your sleep interrupted by something you can do nothing about.

HERE IS THE LESSON

A variation on this ploy, suitable for the thoughtless neighbours whose late-night loud-volume television viewing habits are turning you into a sleepless wreck, is to help them see the error of their ways by waiting for Sunday morning and Radio Four's Morning Service programme. Turn the volume of your radio up as far as it will go, position the speakers for maximum effect, and leave before the first hymn. Put the radio on a timer switch if you're a true Christian. Leave it on all day if not. What better way to make them repent?

GET YOUR OWN BACH

If early morning hymns aren't going to faze them, take a tip from the case of Dorset grandmother Mary Carruthers. In May 1993, after countless complaints from her neighbours, she was found guilty of playing Jim Reeves records 18 hours a day. In a bid to make her stop, the magistrate ordered that her hi-fi be seized and visitors barred between 9 P.M. and 9 A.M.

The lesson? If you want to turn the tables with antisocially sociable neighbours, use your turntable: get hold of the the most "offensive" music you can find (search your local music library for examples)— Jim Reeves, Max Bygraves, or James Last if they're into heavy metal; Guns 'n' Roses, Judas Priest, or AC/DC if Bach is their man—and play it as loud and as long as it takes to put them in a spin and get your message through.

LIVE WIRES

If you're plagued by nonstop ravers, one way to rediscover the sound of silence is by sabotaging the biggest source of noise—the stereo. You can go for a direct attack—supergluing the tape-deck/CD-player door shut or removing the needle or player arm from the record player—or try the more subtle approach of disabling the speakers: stick fine knitting needles through the mesh cover of the speaker cones and poke, poke, poke.

Alternatively, locate their fuse box and simply flip the supply switch off. If the partygoers are supremely pissed, chances are they won't manage to work out what's happened.

SO SOIREE

You can have a lot of fun embarrassing your targets next time they host a genteel drinks evening or dinner party. The trick is to avoid being obvious. Try doctoring the punch-bowl—a handful of salt to help the guests work up a real thirst, or how about a glass of urine if your target has really pissed you off? Or liquid laxative if they've shat on you once too often. Liquid laxative comes into its own, too, if it's a bring-a-plate affair. Go easy on the amount you add, though, as it's powerful stuff. If you've got those chocolate-flavoured laxatives, try adding them to a chocolate mousse or cheesecake, or use one of those chocolate moulding kits to make up a mix of half-laxative and half-chocolate time bombs. Guaranteed to ensure your fellow guests feel an unpleasant gut reaction to their hosts in future.

Cocktail cherries and olives offer a natural hiding place for all sorts of nasties. Try stuffing the cavity with a piece of ultrahot chilli pepper or, if you're a fishing fan, why not delve into the bait box for a handful of maggots and turn your hors-d'oeuvres into horror d'oeuvres.

RAISE A GLASS

Another neat party ploy is to superglue either all the glasses to the table or all the bottles of booze to whatever surface they happen to be standing on. That should definitely slow down the fun.

ADDED EXCITEMENT

If the event is a chi-chi dinner party, go prepared. Secrete a small, blunt piece of broken glass or a small pebble in your pocket. When the main course arrives, begin eating, stop suddenly, choke a little, and bring your napkin up to your mouth. In the process, transfer the glass or pebble to your hand. Look like you're fishing around for something in your mouth, then pull out the glass or pebble.

Look shocked. Pretend to make light of it as your red-faced host sinks through the floor and the rest of the guests suddenly lose their appetites.

PARTY TRICKS

Another good way to ruin someone's party—as just about everybody knows—is to send the hosts the bill, in the shape of the boys in blue, to quiet things down. This works best if you are actually one of the guests, as it not only allows you to witness the results but also gives you a good alibi. The trick is to slip away when things get going and phone the police. You'll be asked to give your name and address, so do your homework beforehand and give them the name of one of your target's neighbours. Now, rejoin the party and wait for the knock on the door.

HACK ATTACK

Start the rumours flying by writing anonymously or in the name of a secondary target to the local newspaper's gossip columnist (or the national dailies, if your target is well-known enough to warrant it). Adopt a moral high tone, and state in your letter that you are appalled to learn that the paper is planning to reveal details of your target's former drug/ alcohol/sex problem. State that it hasn't been a easy path for them in the years since they went clean, and the last thing they need right now is for all to be brought up again. Talk about clean slates, etc., and ask them to give the target a break.

Any paper staffed with journalists worth their salt will check the veracity of the letter, so it might be best to write anonymously, in order that the hacks' first port of call is the target himself. Assuming your target really hasn't got anything to hide, he'll be outraged, and the paper very likely won't print a breath of it for fear of a libel suit. On the other hand, journalists love to gossip—and why let the facts stand in the way of a good story? Your target, meanwhile, will be sweating—wondering how long before his social reputation is ruined, who among his social circle has heard the rumours, and, indeed, who among them started the whole damn thing?

HAPPY BIRTHDAY

Make your target feel really wanted on his birthday with a few surprise deliveries. Order a special birthday cake, champagne, and flowers, and ask for them to be delivered. Throw in a stripper-gram, perhaps, or something especially appropriate and, naturally, find a way to charge it all to your target.

If you want to cause a bit of a stir for your married target on her special day, have a big bunch of flowers delivered to her, along with a card saying something along the lines of *"Flowers for my precious petal"*. This will work especially well if you can organise for the gift to be delivered at a time when you know your target will be involved in a quiet family celebration or an intimate dinner for two.

The stripper-gram mentioned earlier can be used to great effect at posher birthday bashes. Organise the crudest one you can find—a hunky male stripper, perhaps, if your target's male and assumed to be heterosexual (that should give the guests something to speculate about) or a total prude and member of the Mary Whitehouse faction. Of course, the guests will probably find it all rather funny, but unless you've severely underestimated his or her sense of humour, your target should be seethingly embarrassed by the whole thing.

TAKE THE CAKE

Ruin your target's wedding—and cause her social embarrassment—by writing to the caterers to tell them the big day is off and to cancel the food. Leave this hit till the very last minute—a day or two beforehand. Include a few lines about how you realise it is very short notice and that you are willing to foot the entire bill. Ask them to donate the food to the local Salvation Army hostel, and make sure you mention that you would prefer them not to telephone, saying that with all the other arrangements you have to cancel and the distress the situation has caused, you really don't want to be bothered by any more calls than are absolutely necessary.

SAY IT WITH FLOWERS

Going back to that bunch of flowers—you can introduce a host of nasties into your target's life in the guise of a lovely floral arrangement. Try secreting a handful of maggots inside the protective cellophane wrapping of a bouquet, or a nice, hairy spider if your target is arachnophobic, or one of those big, furry caterpillars.

You can also send your best wishes with a pot plant, of course. Add a couple of Andrews tablets to the soil, so that when it is watered it will fizz and bubble alarmingly like acid. Go one step further and dig in a few theatrical fake blood capsules along with the fizzy tablets for a true house-of-horrors effect.

GO WILD

Camping can be great fun and a good way to make friends. Usually a sort of Campers Code operates, to ensure people's privacy and possessions are protected and that help is there when you need it. Sometimes, though, you find the people who've decided to share the great outdoors with you are just plain obnoxious, borrowing equipment without asking, keeping you awake all night with their noise, and fouling the site with their rubbish. One good way to show them how unwelcome they are is to encourage plenty of equally unwelcome guests to pay them a visit, in the form of insects.

You can do this in several ways: send the kids out to collect as many big insects as they can, then release them in one hit inside your target's tent when they're not around; smear meat fat from cooking around their campsite to attract flies, or crush a packet of biscuits and scatter the crumbs to bring in the ants. But if you really want to make them whine, offer to lend them your mosquito "repellent". Mix up a syrup of sugar and lemon juice and pour it into an empty repellent bottle, then stand back as the mosquitoes make a beeline for them.

BE THEIR GUEST

Send out invitations in your targets' name to as many of their acquaintances as you can think of. Don't ask people to reply, simply give a time and date, say it's a casual affair—"just a few people", and ask them to bring a bottle. This way, hopefully, your targets won't get wind of what's going on until the first "guest" turns up to destroy the peace of their quiet Sunday afternoon at home. Even if they do find out, they'll never be able to scotch your scam entirely because they won't know whom you've invited. Invite yourself if you want to witness their discomfort firsthand, but make sure you're not the first to turn up.

A GOOD CRACK

Pull a swift one on your target by buying a Christmas cracker kit and making up your own, complete with "surprise" gifts, such as individual condoms, and, instead of those awful jokes, typewritten messages hinting embarrassingly at adulterous liaisons, sexually transmitted diseases, etc. Pack them in a box, wrap them in suitably Christmassy paper, and send them to your target, without a card, naturally. Of course, the best thing about crackers is that it takes two to pull them, so your target is inevitably going to have some explaining to do.

WAX LYRICAL

While you're feeling crafty, why not invest in a candle-making kit as well? Make up a killer version of those romantic scented candles by adding a dose of melted sulphur to the liquid wax you pour into the mould. When the candles are lit, the room will fill with an overpowering smell of rotten eggs.

No sulphur? Well, powdered iodine will soon smoke them out. How to use them? Well, if you think your boy-friend is showing off his skills in the kitchen as a prelude to his skills in the bedroom with someone other than yourself, you could smuggle a couple into his home or simply present them—but make sure you have a couple of unscented candles with you in case your lover suggests an immediate romantic interlude.

You could also smuggle them into that smoochy candlelit restaurant that refused to acknowledge that its wine was corked, the service nonexistent, and the food inedible.

SEASON'S GREETINGS

If it's the season of goodwill, buy a blank card with a Christmas scene and add your own message, in tacky verse, of course. The effect of a poison-pen letter when it's in the guise of something as innocuous as a Christmas card is twice as potent. Alternatively, bring a secondary target into the picture by signing his or her name to the message.

While you're filled with Christmas spirit, why not send your target a suitable gift: condoms for the devout Catholic family whose horde of rampaging children mean that Sunday is certainly not your day of rest; several indigestion tablets in a pill bottle marked "Penicillin", with the message, "For the woman who now has everything" to the target you know is cheating on her spouse; or a bottle of Diacalm and the message, "For the woman who gives me the shits" to the target who's dumped on you once too often. Use your imagination, and remember, protect yourself by posting your gift from another town or an area you have no connection with.

WHERE THERE'S SMOKE . . .

Is your target a barbecue fanatic? Watch his social aspirations go up in smoke at his next alfresco affair by substituting the following recipe for the charcoal briquettes. Combine 16 parts of sulphur with 12 parts saltpetre and one part finely powdered charcoal. Mix to a paste with a little water and add some plaster powder to make the mixture set. Mould into a briquette and, when almost set, dust with crushed charcoal briquette.

Several of these in your target's barbecue will produce clouds of white smoke—and cast a pall over the proceedings. Throw in some ground red pepper, and you'll reduce your target's guests to tears as well.

FLIGHTS OF FANTASY

If your target's fond of hosting garden parties or is planning to have a garden wedding reception or outdoor party, why not give her a real buzz with a fly past? Depending on your resources, you can either use a model plane and attach a suitably embarrassing message on a banner, or hire the real thing to tow your message of ill-will through the skies for all and sundry to see.

CHAMPAGNE COCKTAIL

We've all heard the old revenge trick of peeing in your target's drink while he's not looking. Well, as my final suggestion, here's a variation on the theme, based on a possibly apocryphal incident involving a famous London chef. Unfortunately, due to the anatomy of the ploy, it's strictly one for the boys.

According to the story, the famous chef was wining and dining a particularly attractive young woman. Sadly for him, though, she was steadfastly resisting his every advance. Eventually, he got the message—but decided if he couldn't have her, he'd have the next best thing: the last laugh. He waited till she slipped off to powder her nose, then grabbed her half-finished glass of champagne, whipped out his willy, dunked it in the glass, and proceeded to use it as a swizzle stick, announcing to the surrounding diners, "Well, that's the closest I'm going to get tonight."

Seconds later the young woman returned to her seat and downed the doctored (or should that be dick-tered?) champagne without suspecting a thing, and the chef went home alone but happy. Just goes to show, doesn't it—where's there's a willy, there's a way.

Travel

*H*olidays are a prime opportunity to send your target packing. If you're travelling abroad with someone who turns out to be an utter creep and you find yourself planning to travel back alone, don't suffer in silence—take action and extend his holiday for him. Pop out to the shops and have a rubber stamp made. Then, next time your tiresome travel companion leaves his bag unattended, stamp "deceased" over every page of his passport. He'll be in dead trouble when he tries to get home. If someone pisses you off, get on his case. Check out these ideas for one that's just the ticket . . .

HOME ALONE

Have you ever been let down by someone who promised to go away on a trip with you and then called it off at the last minute for no very good reason? These insensitive creatures need to learn a lesson, and what better way to pay them back than in kind?

Tell them that you have won a trip for two to Paradise Island (select the destination your targets have dreamed of visiting all their lives). Emphasise the all-expenses-paid nature of the trip, and organise a series of cosy evenings in which you plan all the fabulous things you're going to do. Then, a day or two before "departure day", go off on holiday with someone else. When your targets try to contact you, arrange for your flatmate/family member/ansaphone to inform them that you are in wherever it was you'd planned to go with whomever it is you've actually gone with. Oh, and don't forget to send them a nice postcard.

SUSPICIOUS MINDS

Arranging nonexistant trips for your enemy can be just the thing to send him into orbit. How about a quick call to his wife just before he goes on a business trip? Just ring saying you're the travel agent and tell her that the tickets for Mr Target and (name of secretary or fictitious girlfriend) to Paris/Venice/Vienna are ready to be collected.

CAMPING CARRY-ON

Not everybody's holidays are so glamorous. Camping trips can be pretty hard work, but the rewards are being close to nature and enjoying the peace and quiet . . . until, that is, the Addams Family and their Super Woofer ghetto blaster arrive next door. Try to get into conversation with them. Say that the snakes aren't really a problem because they only come out at night when everyone is inside their tents, all zipped up and snake-proof.

Truly offensive people may deserve rougher treatment. We heard a story about a gang of six lads camping in a large self-groundsheeted tent who thought it was amusing to stay up all night, playing their music really loudly and having belching competitions. Needless to say, they were all pretty pooped the following morning, so they didn't notice when a jeep drew up beside them and the driver, having pulled out their tent pegs, ran a rope through loops where the pegs had been. He then took the boys for a short spin and managed to cover quite a lot of ground and even some water, too. The groundsheeted tent acted as an envelope, and by the time the jeep had stopped and our hungover heroes had managed to find the zip, there was no sign of their tour guide.

FREE WHEELS

It's hard to believe, but some people actually feel ripped off by National Express, British Rail, and other great British public transport organisations. If you're sick of widely advertised bargains which turn out to exist only on the fifth Sunday of the month, introduce a few bargains of your own. Have posters and leaflets printed with the name and logo of your target organisation offering all kinds of discounts. Free and half-price tickets for senior citizens during rush hours can be particularly troublesome and will cost your target company's PR department lots of time and money.

SUNK AND DISORDERLY

Sailing is a gentleman's sport, but, like everything, it attracts its share of jerks. There are a couple of good ways to sink them, though. If your target is a loud and aggressive type who uses his motor yacht like a speedboat, try linking his craft to somebody's private mooring, the more rickety-looking the better. Next time your man blasts off into the blue, he'll be taking somebody else's private property with him—not at all the kind of behaviour the British Yachting Association tends to encourage.

If you know your target's call sign and have use of a marine-band-frequency radio, you can create the impression that his vessel is in distress. It won't be long before the coastguard is at your target's vessel, anxious to know where the fire is, and although he may accept that your target was not responsible for the calls, he will nevertheless want to know why his call sign was used. Needless to say, the coast- guard will be even more impatient if it happens again.

AIRLINES

Air travel offers numerous opportunities to bring a deserving target down to Earth with a bump. For starters, it's easy to cancel a reservation. If your target is going away in high summer and you know the airline he or she is using, one little phone call is all it takes.

Send Them Packing
It may well suit your purpose to ensure your target gets as far as the airport. If you're there when she

checks in, switch the luggage labels and send her stuff on a holiday of its own. Or maybe you should lend a hand with the packing. A bag of suspicious-looking white powder, a wicked-looking knife, a replica gun, or an air pistol are bound to cause comment at security and are never, ever laughed off. If you don't want to put a genuine weapon in the bag, how about just a shape of one cut out of foil? This will show up on the metal detector or X-ray machine, will be difficult to find, and will really annoy the security guards when they find it's a hoax.

Leaving bogus hijack or bomb-planting plans featuring your target and his home/place of work will probably not be taken too seriously but may ensure that he or she is marked down as a potentially dangerous lunatic—information that will, naturally, be passed on to the police.

Metal always sets the alarm bells ringing when it goes through the metal detector, and if that metal turns out to be a tiny, nostril-sized coke spoon, it may well lead to further enquiries.

Highly Amusing
Some of the biggest laughs are to be had by waiting until your target is airborne. If your least-favourite person is travelling on your least-favourite airline, bring them together with a bang. After your target checks in, approach the flight attendant with a note in a sealed envelope addressed to your target and this request: "See that man/woman who just went through? That's my uncle/aunt/husband/wife/son/daughter, and I have a great birthday surprise for him/her. Would you please give him/her

this note when you get airborne? It's all right if everyone wants to sing along. Gosh, s/he's going to be so surprised." The note that your unsuspecting target will open in flight will be one of the following:

- *Please be discreet. If you have any flying experience, come to the front of the aeroplane; the pilot's dead.*

- *This aeroplane has been hijacked and the terrorists have chosen you to be thrown out of the cargo hatch as a symbol. Come to the cockpit or we'll blow up the aeroplane.*

- *A 4-year-old girl/boy has identified you as the person who molested her/him in the airport toilets just before departure. We are holding you for arrest until landing in _____.*

Service with a Smile
Was your flight ruined by a visually challenged flight attendant who couldn't see the light above your seat indicating that you needed attention? Maybe she was one of those maternal figures who knew better than you did that another cup of coffee would only keep you awake. Or perhaps her time was fully taken up discussing her wedding plans with other members of the cabin crew. If you're dissatisfied with your flight attendant, complaining about it during the flight is unlikely to do you any good—in fact, it'll probably make matters worse. And if you write to the airline, your letter will be ignored unless there are at least five other letters with the same complaint—and we all know how lazy people are about complaining once

they've got home. No, what you need is a carefully crafted letter that will attract the attention of the the airline's personnel department, and direct retribution to the right person:

Dear Sir,

I just wanted to thank you for providing flight attendants as friendly and efficient as your Susan Megaslime, on whose flight I was fortunate enough to be travelling the other day.

It had been a long day, and I was feeling anxious and rather edgy. I refused the first three drinks offered, but Ms Megaslime finally forced me to partake and I relaxed very rapidly after that. While I did not really wish to begin drinking (I am a reformed alcoholic), the four drinks I had in transit really did make the flight far more pleasant.
What really impressed me was the fact that Ms Megaslime was able to spot my anxiety despite the fact that she had worked 27 straight hours (she was also quite personable, telling me of the need for some stewardesses to take extra jobs—a concern for me since it is my daughter's ambition).

I'd really like to thank you for making what started out as a horrible trip into a nice one.

Yours sincerely,

When this little time bomb reaches your airline's

personnel department, your friendly stewardess may well find she is taking flight permanently.

Custom-Made

Finally, after an eventful trip, what better way to welcome your target home than with the careful attentions of the customs men? Despite all the publicity about how customs are seizing more drugs that ever, they know that the war on drug smugglers is far from over. This means that any tip-off about an incoming shipment is taken very seriously and no one is above suspicion.

If you want to make your target look a mule, make an anonymous call to the airline or airport to the effect that you know he will be carrying drugs back on (give flight and date). Naturally, this is more credible if your target is on his way home from Amsterdam or the Far East than if he's returning from Salzburg or the Dordogne. However, customs can't afford to ignore a tip-off, and your target will almost certainly receive a thorough searching.

The beauty of this little trick is that the crosser your target becomes, the more suspicious they'll get. What's more, even if they don't find anything, they'll probably keep a file open on your target— just in case.

Work

Cursed by colleagues? Bullied by bureaucrats? Using the memo as ammunition, the briefcase as a bringer of justice, and the photocopier as your front man, wreak your revenge on office officiousness.

There are two main targets in the workplace: irritating individuals who make your working life a misery, and the organisation itself, with its petty policies and vindictive behaviour. Read on for how to control both types of pest.

OUT OF CONTACT

Is your target a journalist, salesman, or someone else who relies heavily on phoning contacts? Here's your chance to teach him to stand on his own two feet. Simply acquire his contact book and, being careful to use the same colour ink, carefully alter a few digits in all the telephone numbers. Stick to those that can be easily changed—3 to an 8, 1 to a 4 or 7, and so on. If he uses an electronic pocket number-and-address directory, a few minutes in a glass of water should flush that memory clean.

LOCK SHOCK

If your target uses one of those combination-lock briefcases, why not shut him out of his own business? If he tends to leave his briefcase lying around open, it's the easiest thing in the world to get in and change that combination. As most people tend to keep the same combination and just slam and scramble it without checking, your target is in big trouble come opening time. This is particularly effective if done just prior his leaving to give an important presentation.

GET THE MESSAGE

One of the most maddening breeds of office pest is the individual who is never at her desk and expects her colleagues to take all her messages in addition to somehow finding time to get on with their own jobs. One way of dealing with this is to take all the messages, pass on about 20 per cent of them, and create a file in the back of her drawer marked "messages". It's unlikely that this will be spotted by someone who is never at her desk, and she will start to miss meetings and fail to return calls and get into big trouble. If she is sensible at this point, she will start to spend more time answering her own phone. If not, well, when the crunch comes, there'll be a big file clearly marked "messages", which anyone who opened her files with any regularity should have found.

PEN FOUNTAIN

Make a blot on your arch-enemy's career by booby-trapping his or her pen. Remove the lid of that oh-so-stylish Mont Blanc fountain pen and pour in a few drops of ink. Don't overdo it; two or three drops will be enough. Keeping the lid upright, replace the pen into the lid, wipe the whole thing clean, and wait for your target to make a big splash at the next meeting.

SEASON TO BE JOLLY

Spread a little Christmas cheer by discreetly leaving a totally unsuitable Christmas present for the boss "from" your target. The Sex Maniac's Diary would probably go down a storm with feminist lady bosses, Arthur Scargill's memoirs with a staunch Tory, and a guide to changing your career with absolutely nobody.

STICK TO BUSINESS

The "tidy desk is a sign of a sick mind" cliché is pretty tired, but there are people who seem to spend more time arranging the objects on their desk than actually working, and most of them are in positions of power (let's face it, what minion has time to arrange his pencil sharpener, letter rack, and stapler in order of size?). Save the company precious time in future desk arrangements by supergluing all these items down—pens and pencils, too. Expensive solid wood desks are particularly effective here.

Maybe this target also has his certificates framed and arranged on the walls. As we all know, either you can do your job or you can't, and anyone who needs to prove to his colleagues that he continued his studies past 16 obviously can't. Help cure him of this unhealthy reliance on meaningless pieces of paper by defacing them with magic marker.

While you're in his office, you could also introduce some extra items. A pair of little girl's flowery knickers sticking out of a desk drawer might arouse curiosity in a fastidious secretary, especially if the office's incumbent doesn't have any school-age children.

STAMP IT OUT

Angry with a sloppy postboy or girl? If this target's job includes licking stamps for the post, try doctoring the stamp sheets. Hairspray is invisible, dries quickly, and tastes absolutely foul. Another problem licked!

HURT GOSSIP

Office gossips fall into several categories. Most are excellent, harmless, and entertaining sources of information, but some are just plain vicious. If you have been the victim of slanderous talk or anonymous letters, you might like to repay someone in kind. Write a really personal, tear-jerking letter "from" the gossip, confessing that the reason she gossips is because her life is so empty. That she envies the young people and wishes that she could have proper friendships without having to invent things all the time. Make it as pathetic as possible, and end it along the lines of, "I have never been deeply religious, but I am begging for your help now, before I do something drastic."

Next, make lots of "original" copies of the letter on a word processor (no photocopies here) and send them out to all the local churches—including the Mormons and Jehovah's Witnesses, lots of newspaper agony aunts, the local MP, doctor, hospital, psychic consultants, crisis centres and any other civic do-gooders. Naturally, the letters should all carry the "sender's" name, address, and telephone number. An additional touch is to send one to a nonexistant church so that it is returned to your target and she can get to see a copy of the letter firsthand. You could also get a few friends to phone and say they got a copy of the letter under their car windscreen wipers in the office carpark, and if there's anything they can do . . .

THANKS FOR THE MEMO

Memos are the lifeblood of bureaucrats. Their purpose is usually to make demands and comments that even the most obsessive bureaucrat would find too petty and embarrassing to make to your face. Even so, as such, they can be used to your advantage. Memos are easy to intercept. They tend to sit around in filing trays waiting to be picked up by postboys and girls, so why not purloin your target's, hold on to it for a couple of days, and then return it with a few withering comments scribbled on it —initialled, of course, by one of the big cheeses. Alternatively, you may want to destroy the outgoing or the response memo, or send copies of sensitive memos to the wrong people.

Internal post envelopes are also wonderful weapons. Mostly they work on the recycling principle of crossing off the name of the last user and read-dressing. You can make a vicious and insulting anonymous memo to one target appear to be sent from another, therefore, just by filling in and crossing out in the appropriate place.

GET A JOB

If you really hate working with your target, perhaps you should help him or her to find a new job. Strategically-placed CVs belonging to your target (genuine or made-up) left around the office photocopier should soon set tongues wagging. Alternatively, applying for lots of jobs in a similar area of business in your target's name will also attract attention, especially if you list the target's current boss as a referee. You may also wish to enumerate your reasons for leaving—including the unprofessional behaviour of your boss and the unethical way in which the company conducts its business. If you're applying to a competitor, it's unlikely they'll keep your revelations to themselves.

While you're working on this tack, send out a press release to your trade's magazine announcing your target's appointment to a post with a rival firm. You'll need to acquire some headed notepaper for your rival firm—easily done by just writing to them with any old enquiry, typing out your release, and combining the two in the photocopier. Stick to known facts about your target—age, family status, "former" job—and wait for press day. Despite your victim's best reassurances, the big cheese will probably suspect that some dopey PR just sent the release out too early, and your target will be treated with great suspicion.

If your victim ever does get as far as a genuine interview and you find out who it's with, throw a spanner in the works by phoning up as your target and rearranging the time for an hour earlier. It doesn't look good changing an interview time anyway, and when you then show up late . . .

Alternatively, you could put the frighteners on a useless colleague by advertising his or her job in the trade press. Every profession has its own appointments pages where everyone in the business looks to see what's going on and who's going where. What a surprise it'll be for your target to be browsing through the appointments and find his own up for grabs.

DOUBLE DEALER

Use corporate paranoia to destroy your target's career. Say, for example, your target works for Eastern Adhesives in Norwich, whose main competitors are Southern Superglue in Portsmouth and Western Weld-Tight in Wolverhampton. In your target's name, drop a line to an actual senior executive at Southern Superglue, but on the envelope put the name down as Southern Superglue and put Western Weld-Tight's Wolverhampton address underneath. Of course, the postman will be unable to find a Southern Superglue in Wolverhampton, so the letter will be returned to the address on the back of the envelope—that of Eastern Adhesives. It will probably be opened by a secretary trying to find the right department for it, but when she sees the contents it will go straight to the boss. Why? Well, your letter will read as follows:

Mr Fred Bloggs
Product Development Director
Southern Superglue

Dear Fred,

Please forward the £10,000 payment we agreed upon last month for the new formula and product specs I furnished you with. As you know, I have put myself and the future of the company I work for at serious risk to be of help to you. I expect a cheque for the agreed sum, made out to my 10-year-old daughter, to be with me by return of post. We had a deal, remember?

This will ensure your target has masses of explaining to do, and the mix-up with the two competitors' addresses will make those in charge think he was dealing double. If your target is one of those who is always trying to get the boss's attention, this little number will be the answer to his prayers.

PROS AND CONS

Call your target's boss and announce yourself as so-and-so from the borough probation unit. Say that you wish to confirm that the target does actually work there. Then ask whether she has been behaving normally. Does she disappear at lunchtime and come back with large amounts of money? Or does she have any contact with children in the course of a normal working day?

BAD COMPANY

If it's the company itself that you're angry with, there are dozens of ways to commit petty but rewarding bits of vandalism and spread damaging disinformation. Naturally, many of these are best performed after you've organised your next job move.

If you work in a business where you have telephone contact with the public, you're bound to have experienced the bitchy call. Should you find yourself at the end of the phone to something that sounds like Margaret Thatcher with PMT, give her your name—well, okay, your boss'—and let fly a string of abuse. It's simple, effective, and therapeutic.

THE EYE HAS IT

If you have any genuine stories relating to your company regarding corruption, abuse of power, or just plain stupid behaviour, send them anonymously to *Private Eye*. The *Eye* may try to verify it, but it is known for printing stories provided they have what it calls "the ring of truth". This excellent publication is read by all MPs and captains of industry and, while many may claim they don't believe a word of it, they all do. You can be sure that if a story appears in *Private Eye*, the people at the top of your organisation will be very worried indeed.

OLD BILL OF HEALTH

Employers also hate visits from the Health and Safety department or the fire department. An anonymous tip-off from a concerned employee should soon get someone round checking your employer's most private nooks and crannies. There's an excellent chance there'll be at least a couple of things wrong, which will be expensive and will perhaps even involve a hearing. If not, you can always ensure the inspectors don't waste their journey by tampering with the dates of service on the fire extinguishers and padlocking the safety doors just before the visit. And what's bad for your boss' health is good for yours.

POLITICALLY INCORRECT

Companies are all trying terribly hard to be politically correct these days. The prospect of being accused of any of the isms—sexism, racism, even ageism, quite rightly turns personnel departments cold. Well, it can be expensive if you get taken to court, you see. So any company that advertised for an "attractive female secretary, aged 18-25, white applicants preferred", would probably attract the attention of any number of angry pressure groups—if someone sent them a copy of it. But who on earth would place an ad like that in these enlightened times?

HACKED OFF

If you're leaving a company that uses computers, the damage that can be wrought is immense. If you're really clever with computers, you could try introducing a time-bomb virus—a couple of years ago some hackers managed to create a "Friday the Thirteenth" virus, which wiped clean many people's hard disks on that particular day. Another game might be to get rid of important software or, on your last day, delete loads of important files. If you have a hated colleague's password, so much the better. Another good trick is to stick a powerful magnet on the bottom of an important floppy-disk file box. The company will not be looking for this and will probably spend a fortune on extra disks before replacing the computer, all to no avail. What a flop!

VIDEO NASTY

The *Sun* newspaper recently devoted a whole page to Paul, who was leaving his job at an electrical shop, and his last-day frolics with a stripper-gram girl. The three-minute video of Paul's farewell surprise—which featured him licking whipped cream off his visitor's breasts and having his bare backside spanked with a leather whip—somehow ended up in a camcorder, which was then sold. The new owners were horrified enough to complain to the shop and accept compensation, though fortunately they were not too embarrassed to tell the whole story to the *Sun*, which ran the pictures large. It's just a story, but it makes you realise that somebody must really have disliked Paul quite a lot. Happy filming!

BOG STANDARDS

Office loos are a fun target for the disgruntled employee. Nobody likes grotty toilet facilities, and your employers will have to put up with no end of complaints. Try substituting the liquid soap in the dispenser with vehicle axle grease, clear casting resin (without the hardener added), stale chicken fat, emulsion paint, or dye.

As for the loos, quick-bonding superglue applied to the bottom of the seat and the seat cover in each of the stalls will certainly cause panic after lunch, as will varnish, photocopier toner powder (impossible to remove) or paint applied to similarly coloured toilet seats.

TAKE THE RISE

You can put lifts out of action by taking the lift to the top floor and supergluing a thin slice of hard wood or metal into the runner channel to wedge the doors open, before legging it downstairs to your relevant floor.

FAN CLUB

Finally, if your company uses ceiling fans in the summer in its boardrooms, balance a couple of small bottles of opened ink on the still fan blades, near the center axis, just prior to an important meeting. As soon as someone touches that button, you'll hear the splatter of impatient feet as your company's valued clients make a dash for the door.